LDS missionaries are coming
with the good news that faith
fills a major void in equipping ....
the Mormon Missionary Message is the apologetic scouting report
you need to converse effectively with Latter-day Saints. Through a
variety of capable contributors, you get a play-by-play of the Mormon
missionary lessons and get coached in how to respond to each. The
young missionaries who visit your door need you to read this!

Dr. Bryan Hurlbutt

Lead pastor of Lifeline Community in West Jordan, Utah, author of
Tasty Jesus, and contributor to *Sharing the Good News with Mormons*

For the Christian who wants to better communicate with those
Mormons who come to their doors, as well as with their Mormon
friends and family members, this resource will prove to be an educa-
tional primer in considering the fundamental concepts of Mormonism.
This, in turn, will equip readers to respond by sharing the biblical
gospel of grace with *truth in love* (Ephesians 4:15).

Eric Johnson

Cohost of *Viewpoint on Mormonism*, research associate with Mormon
Research Ministry (MRM.org), and author of several books on
Mormonism, including *Sharing the Good News with Mormons*,
Introducing Christianity to Mormons, and *Mormonism 101*

I loved this book! Not only do we get inspiring stories of God's grace
as He draws and redeems the authors out of Mormonism and into
life in Christ, but we also get a very straightforward explanation of
Christian doctrines that counter the teachings of LDS missionaries. There is a lot of wisdom here for the compassionate Christian
who wants to be effective in witnessing to the Mormon missionary,
returned missionary, or their LDS neighbor. I rejoiced to see the authors
walk us through why confrontational evangelism doesn't work with
those whose version of history is that they are a persecuted people.
I would recommend this book for every church pastor or layperson
who wants to understand how to reach Mormons with the gospel.
I would also recommend this book for those in the process of leaving Mormonism and taking their first steps into historic, orthodox,
biblical Christianity.

Dr. Paul Robie

Founding pastor of Utah's largest church, South Mountain
Community Church

As former LDS members and missionaries, the authors respectfully share from their own experiences how the Mormon missionary program is structured, as well as provide insights on various differences between Mormonism and biblical Christianity. I recommend this book to anyone seeking to better understand and talk with their LDS friends.

Sandra Tanner
President of Utah Lighthouse Ministry and (along with her late husband, Jerald Tanner) author of nearly forty books on Mormonism, including *Mormonism—Shadow or Reality?* She is a great-great-granddaughter of Brigham Young, the second president of the Mormon Church

This book portrays the day-to-day cultural experiences, including the struggles, of Mormon missionaries and compares the LDS doctrines they teach with those communicated in the Bible. Written largely by former LDS missionaries who are now biblical Christians, they have been on both sides of the fence. This is an excellent resource for Christians who desire to understand and witness to Mormon missionaries. One of the best features is the description of each missionary discussion in fine detail. Readers should discover insights that enable them to have fruitful discussions with LDS missionaries.

Dr. Lynn Wilder
Founder of Ex-Mormon Christians United for Jesus, cohost of *Unveiling Grace Podcast*, former BYU professor, and author or coauthor of several books on Mormonism and the Christian faith, including *Unveiling Grace, 7 Reasons We Left Mormonism,* and *Leaving Mormonism*

This is the perfect book for any Christian who wants to understand his Mormon neighbors. In *Responding to the Mormon Missionary Message*, those who have never been LDS have the opportunity to hear from those who have walked in the missionaries' shoes. From growing up in the religion to being trained to spread the religion, these authors have the experiential authority needed to describe the perspective of those who are practicing Mormonism. Even better is that now, as true believers in Christ and His gospel of grace, these authors help the reader understand how to respond to Latter-day Saints with truth in love. This unique volume deserves its own place alongside other Christian books on Mormonism that have been written through the years.

Jeremy Howard
Staff pastor at Orchard Hills Bible Church in Payson, UT

Responding
to the
Mormon Missionary Message

Responding
to the
Mormon Missionary Message

*Confident Conversations
with Mormon Missionaries
(and Other Latter-day Saints)*

Corey Miller & Ross Anderson
(with other contributors)

We enjoy hearing from our readers. Please contact
us at www.anekopress.com/questions-comments
with any questions, comments, or suggestions.

Responding to the Mormon Missionary Message
© 2023 by Corey Miller and Ross Anderson
All rights reserved. Published 2023.

Cover Designer: Jonathan Lewis
Editor: Paul Miller

Aneko Press

www.anekopress.com
Aneko Press, Life Sentence Publishing, and our logos are trademarks of
Life Sentence Publishing, Inc.
203 E. Birch Street
P.O. Box 652
Abbotsford, WI 54405

RELIGION / Christianity / Church of Jesus Christ of Latter-day Saints
Paperback ISBN: 978-1-62245-933-9
eBook ISBN: 978-1-62245-934-6
10 9 8 7 6 5 4 3 2 1
Available where books are sold

Contents

Register This New Book

Benefits of Registering*

- ✓ FREE **replacements** of lost or damaged books

- ✓ FREE **audiobook** – *Pilgrim's Progress,* audiobook edition

- ✓ FREE information about new titles and other **freebies**

www.anekopress.com/new-book-registration

*See our website for requirements and limitations.

Introduction

If you are reading this, then you almost certainly have seen, and perhaps have spoken with, "Mormon missionaries." More than half of all Americans know an active member of the Church of Jesus Christ of Latter-day Saints (LDS). Their neighbors know them as great neighbors and hardworking, generous people who serve others. They are also known as a proselytizing people. Some sixty-five thousand LDS missionaries are actively seeking to draw converts from other faiths (or no faith). In fact, 30 percent of LDS Church members are converts to the Church. Two-thirds of all Americans have been approached by LDS missionaries at some time. Members of traditional Christian churches are not exempt. Indeed, the majority of LDS converts have some kind of Christian background. The message of the Mormon missionaries contains terms that are common in the Christian world – words such as sin, salvation, faith, repentance, heaven, Jesus, God, etc. – yet have very different meanings. The claims LDS missionaries make to prospective converts depend heavily on the prospective converts having some basic awareness of the Bible.

Despite the familiarity of language and themes, the LDS Church understands God, humanity, salvation, and eternity very differently from historic, biblical Christianity. For example, Latter-day Saints believe that God is an exalted human with a physical body. By contrast, Christianity teaches that God is an infinite spirit who has always been God. Like Mormonism, traditional Christianity identifies Jesus Christ and the Holy Spirit as divine persons. But unlike Mormons, Christians believe that there is only one God (not three) who exists eternally in three distinct persons.

The LDS Church views human beings as literal spirit children of God the Father who have the potential to become gods themselves one day. By contrast, biblical Christianity teaches that humans are creatures (created beings) of God. We can be adopted as God's children by faith, but we are a completely different kind of being than God.

Latter-day Saints see Adam and Eve's sin in Eden as a courageous act that allowed human beings to fulfill their larger destiny, yet the Bible portrays their sin as an utter disaster for humanity. The Bible teaches that instead of having the potential for divinity, human beings are hopelessly lost and fallen and are in desperate need of deliverance and new life.

The Bible consistently presents the death of Jesus on the cross as a sacrifice that pays the entire penalty of sin for all those who trust in His provision. All the benefits of Jesus's atonement – including forgiveness, new life, righteousness, resurrection, and heaven – are ours by God's grace alone, to be received by faith alone. By contrast, Latter-day Saints believe that the death of Christ is necessary, but not sufficient. Faithful Mormons must live up to a long list of extrabiblical (outside of the Bible) commandments and ordinances in order to be considered worthy of being right with God.

Latter-day Saints believe that in the next life, all human beings will be assigned to one of three levels of heaven. Those who meet all of God's requirements will earn the highest level of heaven, where they can create eternal families and become gods. While scripture does speak of our rewards in heaven (1 Corinthians 3:12-14, Matthew 19:28; 25:14-30, 2 John 1:8, etc.), Christians believe that only those who trust in Jesus alone will receive eternal life and what Mormons are taught is very different from what the Bible teaches. And sadly, those who reject Jesus will face God's righteous judgment for their sin and will be eternally separated from God in hell.

These opposing ideas about God, humanity, and salvation are rooted in two different views of truth and authority. Latter-day Saints accept several books as scripture in addition to the Bible, and they believe that God continues to reveal Himself through modern prophets. For Christians, the Bible stands alone as the final authority for faith and life and is the final test of what is true.

Many of these significant differences are glossed over by LDS missionaries, who seek to build a bridge to adherents of other faiths by presenting "milk" before "meat." The differences are also often obscured by the fact that the LDS Church stands for many of the same lifestyle values as biblical Christianity. Both groups value marriage, family, honesty, chastity, community, and other admirable qualities. Latter-day Saints also practice many activities that are familiar to Christians, such as prayer, scripture reading, Sunday church, fasting, and serving. Christians can applaud Mormons for their way of life. However, as you will see as you read this book, while those values and practices look biblical, they are driven by a very different motive and world view.

At the heart, LDS practices flow out of a system that requires worthiness for salvation. While these practices might of themselves be commendable, they represent an unbiblical approach to life because they are motivated by a compulsion to earn God's favor rather than out of a heart of love for God (*If you love Me, keep My commandments.* – John 14:15). In short, as you read this book, you will see many points of LDS doctrine that are clearly not biblical, despite familiar terminology. You will also see many lifestyle aspects that mirror biblical values, but that express a non-biblical understanding of life and salvation.

We wrote this book as a resource for three related audiences. First, we want to provide a resource for any Christians who are interested in comparing Mormonism to historic, biblical Christianity. This book clearly sets forth that comparison. Second, we want to equip Christians who encounter Mormon missionaries. In these pages, Christians will gain the knowledge and discernment they need to resist Mormon conversion tactics, and they will also be equipped to share the biblical gospel with those missionaries. Third, we want to encourage any Christians who know Latter-day Saints, whether missionaries or not. The reality is that any active Mormon is likely to have served an LDS mission, so this book will help any Christian gain wisdom and confidence to engage in meaningful faith conversations with LDS neighbors and friends.

Few Christians feel either motivated or equipped for those faith conversations, but this doesn't have to be the case. I (Ross) was consulting recently with a woman in a Bible-belt state about bringing resources to her church to help the members of her church understand Mormonism and equip them to engage Mormons. She was dismayed that people in her church were unwilling to engage the growing number of Mormons living in their community. This is a common response. Mormon missionaries can come across as confident and well-rehearsed. It can feel intimidating to talk with them about our beliefs and theirs. That is where this book can help.

LDS missionaries seem impossible to reach with the gospel. Young LDS missionaries are indoctrinated into their cause. Their thinking and activities are tightly controlled. Yet there is reason for hope. More and more missionaries are hearing the good news of Jesus while on their missions, from the same people they are trying to reach. Many of them are secretly open to what they hear. It may not be until they return home and reenter a less-structured environment that they have freedom to process what they have heard, but seeds sown during a mission often bear fruit in later life. This is evidenced by the testimony of the former missionaries who contributed to this book. We trust that their stories will encourage and motivate Christians to engage with LDS missionaries, and to prepare themselves to do so well.

This book, though, is not just about learning how to respond to LDS truth claims. It also models how to treat the missionaries (and other Latter-day Saints) who cross our paths. Many missionaries report that the only interaction they had with Bible-believing Christians while on their missions was negative. They were mocked, insulted, turned away, and yelled at, but were never engaged with grace. So many Mormon missionaries complete their missionary service without ever having a constructive faith conversation with a traditional Christian.

This is why it is important to note that every contributor to this book is a former Latter-day Saint who has embraced the biblical Christian faith. We can share firsthand both the knowledge and the experience necessary in order to interact fruitfully with LDS missionaries.

The first section of the book addresses general issues that inform our conversations with Latter-day Saints. Ross Anderson opens by explaining how LDS culture influences how Mormons hear the good news we share with them. Corey Miller then explores the challenge of sharing truth when Latter-day Saints look to personal experience as the ultimate spiritual authority for their beliefs. Matt Wilder increases our empathy by sharing from personal experience a glimpse of what daily life is like for a Mormon missionary.

The second part of the book interacts chapter by chapter with the five lessons in the LDS missionary manual called *Preach My Gospel.* This manual clarifies the core teaching of Mormonism by spelling out what Mormons want potential converts to understand and accept. This makes Part 2 a valuable resource for you whether you are talking to missionaries or to Latter-day Saints in general. Because each of the five contributors in this section served a proselytizing mission for the LDS Church, each chapter offers proven, practical wisdom about how to share God's truth with Latter-day Saints with gentleness and respect.

The standard Bible version used in this book is the New King James Version. The LDS Church officially uses the King James Version, so quotations from LDS sources will reflect that usage. Yet the King James Version is hard to read for many people, and the unfamiliar language often obscures clarity. On the other hand, many Mormons are unfamiliar or uncomfortable with modern-language translations. Thus, we have adopted the New King James Version as our standard Bible version in this book. We think this is a good solution for faith conversations with Latter-day Saints because it bridges the gap between the King James Version and contemporary versions.

While the Church of Jesus Christ of Latter-day Saints is commonly known as the Mormon Church, Latter-day Saints prefer the official title. This is cumbersome for both the writer and the reader. Their preferred shortened form is "The Church of Jesus Christ," yet in our minds, this implies an exclusive status that we cannot grant. As an alternative, we will refer to "the LDS Church" in most cases. At times, we will use the terms "Mormon" or "LDS" as adjectives to refer to the Church and to elements of the culture that it creates. We will also use "Mormon" as a noun to refer to the people themselves. Although this is the common approach long used by major media outlets, and by the LDS Church itself, the LDS Church announced in 2018 that the term "Mormon" is no longer acceptable. Thus, many Latter-day Saints object to the term and see it as promoting negative stereotypes about them. Our motive is not to label or marginalize Latter-day Saints, but simply to provide stylistic variation in keeping with long-established usage. We mean no disrespect and never use any of this terminology in a pejorative sense.

Along the same lines, we have strived in this volume to present LDS views with accuracy and fairness and to represent Mormonism as it is currently believed.

Chapter 1

Clued In to Culture: Engaging Mormons with Discernment

By Ross Anderson

Having faith conversations with Latter-day Saints – missionaries or otherwise – requires a good grasp of the basics of the biblical gospel and how biblical truth relates to LDS claims. The authors in this volume provide such insight as they interact with the core doctrines represented in the LDS missionary lessons. However, one important factor in sharing God's good news with Mormons goes beyond doctrine and apologetics. For biblical truth claims to land in the LDS soul, our conversations need to take into account the Mormon culture, how this culture shapes the Latter-day Saint identity, and the influence it has on how Latter-day Saints hear and evaluate truth.

What Is Culture?

Every human being is embedded in a culture. Culture "includes all the ways in which people perceive and organize material goods, ideas, and values; it embraces the ways in which people interact in society as well as a person's substitutes for God and His revelation."[1] Born and reared into our own culture, we may not be aware of how it affects us. Most of us see our own culture as normative, so the cultural reality we experience becomes reality for us. Thoughtful Christians realize that the unchanging gospel of Jesus Christ takes shape in many different expressions in different cultural settings around the world and over time. In fact, Jesus was born in a particular cultural setting that was very different from the cultures of most followers of Christ today. I have had the privilege of worshipping with followers of Christ in several different countries. Each experience involved different languages, music, formats, and venues. We all worshipped the same Lord Jesus Christ, but each situation reflected a different human culture.

Mormonism as a Cultural Identity

The Church of Jesus Christ of Latter-day Saints is a religion based on a unique belief system, but Latter-day Saints are not just people who believe certain things. Shaped by a common history and life experience, the LDS Church has birthed a unique culture and identity. One LDS scholar writes that "Mormons still think of themselves as a people as much as a church."[2] Based on common beliefs and worldview, the Mormon culture takes shape in all the ways any culture does. Latter-day Saints partake of shared customs, values, and lifestyle. They have a particular vocabulary and folklore. They share distinctive rituals and practices. They have unique art, architecture, and music. The culture of Mormonism defines life for its people. It teaches them what is real, what matters, how to handle life situations, and more. Mormons always

---

1   David J. Hesselgrave, *Communicating Christ Cross-Culturally* (Grand Rapids: Zondervan, 1991), 188.

2   Richard Lyman Bushman, *Mormonism: A Very Short Introduction* (New York: Oxford University Press, 2008), 102.

know what is expected of them because of the norms of their culture. (This includes the expectation that young men will serve as missionaries for the LDS Church.)

People enter the LDS cultural community in two ways: by birth or by conversion. Converts to the LDS Church take on their new identity first by embracing the LDS message and then by adopting the related lifestyle and values. Those born into the Church move through a series of stages or events that reinforce their unique identity – such as baptism at age eight, initiation into the LDS priesthood (for males) at age twelve, a special patriarchal blessing as a teenager, serving a mission as a young adult, and eventually, temple marriage.

Even within the tight-knit LDS culture, not all Mormons are the same. For example, a member of the LDS Church might be "active" or "inactive." Among active Mormons, some are "true believers" and others are closet doubters. Members raised in the Church are different in many ways from converts. Those living in the LDS heartland are different from those who live where Mormons are a minority. Younger members experience Mormon beliefs and practices differently than older members. Different segments of the LDS population define the meaning of their church membership in different ways, yet significant shared elements of a common culture remain.

With that in mind, consider seven broadly typical aspects of LDS culture:

1. Latter-day Saints are very family oriented. They believe that families can be together for eternity. In fact, the family is the key unit of eternal salvation. Traditional family values are important, as are family-centered practices such as weekly Family Home Evening and family reunions.

2. LDS culture promotes personal achievement. Mormons typically are self-reliant, have a strong work ethic, and are driven to personal advancement. This is shaped by

key factors in LDS theology and history, but also by the missionary experience. Missionaries work hard and follow a disciplined regimen.

3. Mormons tend to be socially and politically conservative. Most American Mormons are Republican. They differ from the norm of American society by being more conservative about such issues as marriage, sexual ethics, and illegal drug use.

4. Mormons practice unique dietary restrictions. A policy called the Word of Wisdom sets them apart from most Americans by prohibiting use of alcohol, tobacco, coffee, and tea.

5. History and heritage are very important to Latter-day Saints. They see themselves as part of an important sacred narrative. They feel a strong connection to their forebears.

6. Mormons are fiercely loyal to their Church and its leaders. In their view, the LDS Church is the only true and living church on earth. Its leaders are divinely appointed prophets, so they show great reverence toward their prophets – both living and dead. Any critique of their leaders or their Church is seen as an attack.

7. Latter-day Saints can be very insular. Most of them do not know many non-Mormons. As an all-encompassing community, Mormonism meets the social and relational needs of its members and demands a great deal of their time and energy. As a result, Mormons are rarely well-informed about other faiths. They often see members of other churches as "junior varsity" Christians. They want traditional Christians to see their faith in a positive light, and they are probably interested in converting you to Mormonism, yet they most likely expect you to attack their beliefs. (By the way, one

of the most common ways Latter-day Saints interact with non-Mormons is on their missions. This is often the only substantial interaction Mormons will have with evangelical Christians. How you treat them will either reinforce or break down their stereotypes of Christians.)

We will soon consider how the cultural traits of Mormonism affect our witness to them, but first, let's zoom out and think about how culture relates to faith-sharing in general.

The Unchanging Gospel in Changing Settings

The good news of God's saving grace toward humanity, expressed through the person and work of Jesus Christ, is universal and unchanging. Apart from Christ, every human being is alienated from God and needs Jesus's redemptive work. No one is made right with God except by trusting in Christ – His perfect life, His death, and His resurrection from the dead. These principles are true in every cultural setting.

Yet when Jesus told His followers to *make disciples of all nations* (Matthew 28:18-20), inherent in this commission is a recognition that people with different national identities will hear the good news through different grids. Every human culture has what it considers normal and credible forms of communication. Every culture has unique ways of thinking about important issues such as what is true and what is not (and how to tell the difference), the nature and predicament of humanity, and the nature of the supernatural world. Whenever we communicate the gospel across a cultural divide (large or small), we must take the culture of our audience into account so that the message will actually be heard.

This process is called "contextualization." One Christian missionary scholar describes it like this: "The idea of contextualization is to frame the gospel message in language and communication forms appropriate and meaningful to the local culture and to focus the message upon crucial issues in the lives of the people."[3] The most obvious example of this is the use of language. Whenever we learn a language to share the gospel with people of another nationality, we are adapting to that culture. That is an obvious form of contextualization, but even if our audience speaks English, wisdom suggests other ways that we take a person's culture into account.

This practice of contextualization has biblical precedent in the ministry of the apostle Paul. Acts 13:16-42 tells of Paul speaking in a Jewish synagogue in Pisidian Antioch. He started with the Jewish scriptures and made a case for their fulfillment in Jesus as the Messiah. Later, in Acts 14:8-20, Paul addressed a rural pagan audience in Lystra. He didn't begin by quoting Jewish scriptures because the Old Testament would have been completely foreign to his audience. Instead, he opened with something they had experienced: the general goodness of God in creation. Then, in Acts 17:16-31, Paul addressed a sophisticated pagan audience in the city of Athens. He started with their general religious sentiment, as seen in their altar "to the unknown God," quoting their own authors to connect with their thinking. From there he built a bridge to Jesus and His resurrection. Paul used a different approach in each of these three examples. He wisely communicated in a way appropriate to each specific cultural setting.

Paul understood that when we tell others about Jesus Christ, who He is, and what He has done, we should be discerning about the culture of our audience. We should give thought as to how to start the conversation and what forms of communication and persuasion we should use. This applies whether we are talking to Latter-day Saints or to anyone else. At least in part, our witness is dictated by their culture.

---

3   Sherwood Lingenfelter, *Transforming Culture: A Challenge for Christian Mission*, 2nd ed. (Grand Rapids: Baker, 1998), 12-13.

Sharing the Gospel within the LDS Culture

Traditionally, Christians have engaged Latter-day Saints without much thought for the LDS cultural identity. We have empha- sized comparative doctrine, which is vitally important, but we have not paid much attention to cultural factors that strongly influence how our message is heard. Most Mormons did not join the LDS Church because of doctrinal considerations. The vast majority became Latter-day Saints because they were born into the culture. Others joined for emotional and relational reasons. When we limit our witness to simply comparing truth claims, we ignore much of what matters to Mormons themselves. Let us then explore some specific examples of how LDS cultural traits might affect how we share our faith with them.

To begin with, Latter-day Saints determine truth by expe- rience. They are taught to seek a spiritual experience as the ultimate way to validate their beliefs or to confirm a course of action. As Chapter 2 explains, this subjective experience trumps objective facts and rational arguments. In response, wisdom suggests that we should share truth using the language of experience. For example, my LDS friend and I might debate at length about the doctrine of the Trinity, but I don't want to leave the conversation just at the level of competing ideas. I also want to communicate the emotional impact of that truth in my experience. I might explain that when I think of a God who is so far above my comprehension, I feel a deep sense of awe. I am moved to bow down in humility and offer profound worship to this infinite Being.

Latter-day Saints are also very sensitive to perceived per- secution. Remembering the wrongs committed generations ago against their ancestors, they see themselves as an abused minority. Therefore, any criticism, even mild disagreement, can be construed as an attack against them and their faith. I believe that LDS missionaries are particularly prone to this persecution complex because they stand out as an easy target and experience plenty of rejection. In my conversations with Mormons, I try to stay calm and civil, avoiding any tone of voice that sounds aggressive or disagreeable. I aim to treat missionaries with kindness and generosity.

Mormonism creates a close-knit sense of community, shaped by the early experience of Latter-day Saints as a countercultural society. For decades, the strategy of the LDS Church was to gather converts into a centralized "Zion" where they lived together in isolation from non-Mormons rather than to leave them in the social settings where they were converted. This has created a strong social identity and sense of belonging. When talking to Mormons about Jesus, I am always aware of the difficult challenge they will encounter if they leave their community and family behind to adopt a biblical faith.

Most Christian churches have some kind of statement of faith that spells out basic beliefs in an orderly outline. In Mormonism, though, truth is structured in terms of stories. Latter-day Saints learn the core precepts of their faith by retelling foundational stories that illustrate important truths. For example, the idea that God the Father has a body, and the related notion that He is a distinct being from Jesus, are both rooted in the story of the "First Vision" – Joseph Smith's initial encounter with God. The centrality of stories in the LDS faith invites us to share God's truth in story form as well. After all, the Bible itself is a narrative, not a textbook of systematic theology.

Let me suggest three ways to adapt the message to this narrative approach. First, open the Bible with your LDS friend and read stories from Jesus's life, exploring the implications of what Jesus said and how He acted. Second, learn to share the gospel as God's great story rather than as just a series of logical statements. The story starts with God's good creation, followed by humanity's fall into sin. Then it moves on to God's redemptive work in sending a Savior, and it comes to a climax in the ultimate future renewal of all things. Third, think of ways to express your own personal story of God's work in your life – not just in coming to salvation, but also in His ongoing leading, care, and provision.

Finally, Mormonism is driven by activity, not theology. It is a practical, lived religion. Most Latter-day Saints are not very interested in debates about God or eternity. Missionaries may be an exception because their full-time work is to have faith conversations, but generally, Mormons are interested in how to live out their faith. This creates opportunities for fruitful conversations because the LDS lifestyle is challenging. Mormons are on a continual quest to prove themselves worthy by obeying hundreds of biblical *and* extrabiblical commandments in everyday life. The LDS culture creates tremendous pressure to be perfect – or at least to project an LDS image of perfection. The emphasis on achievement can be exhausting and defeating. I find it more fruitful to steer gospel conversations away from abstract theological topics and toward the personal need many Latter-day Saints feel to find relief from this pressure.

Some Latter-day Saints believe they are living up to the standards, but many know that they fall short. They need to experience grace. When the wheels come off in their lives, they aren't likely to turn to other Latter-day Saints for encouragement. To do so would reveal their weakness and expose them to disrespect and gossip. However, they will often turn to a trusted Christian friend who offers unconditional acceptance. Because LDS missionaries work in pairs, this kind of vulnerability is unlikely – at least while on their mission. But as you invest in building a friendship with the Latter-day Saint in your neighborhood or workplace, you might be that trusted confidant at just the right time.

In the chapters that follow, you will learn a great deal about Latter-day Saint beliefs and claims, as well as how to answer them with biblical truth. But whether you encounter missionaries at your door or LDS friends in your daily life, understanding LDS culture will help you discern how to share the good news of Jesus in ways that sound like good news to them.

* * * *

Ross Anderson, DMin, was born in Utah and was raised LDS. After leaving Mormonism as a young adult, he pursued a Master of Divinity degree and a Doctor of Ministry degree. Anderson has served as a church planter and pastor in Utah for four decades and is currently a teaching pastor at Alpine Church. He is the executive director of Utah Advance Ministries and the founder of the Faith after Mormonism project and the *Culture-Wise* podcast. Ross has authored various books, including *Understanding the Book of Mormon, Understanding Your Mormon Neighbor,* and *Jesus without Joseph* – a study guide for former Mormons. Ross is an avid cyclist and reader. He and his wife, Sally, are parents to five adult children.

Part 1

Meet the Mormons

Chapter 2

Mormon Authority: The Testimony and Mormon Scriptures

By Corey Miller

"For us, authority is everything," quipped Robert Millet, one of the most influential professors at Brigham Young University, the flagship school of "the Church."[4] The Church of Jesus Christ of Latter-day Saints (members are often called "LDS" or "Mormons") claims to be the one true church. They say that it is the only church or movement of God alive today with the proper priestly authority as God's representative on earth. But what does Dr. Millet mean? From its origin and corporate governance to the individually grounded conviction, authority is pervasive throughout every stratum of LDS life.

The Mormon religion depends on two necessary and jointly sufficient assumptions, without which it cannot get off the tarmac. First, they claim that there was a "total apostasy" from the truth in the first century. This doesn't mean that there were no

---

4   Robert Millet, "Authority Is Everything," in *Talking Doctrine: Mormons and Evangelicals in Conversation*, eds. Richard Mouw and Robert Millet (Downers Grove: InterVarsity Press, 2015), 170-176.

adherents professing themselves as "Christian," but it simply means that with the death of the last apostle, the priestly authority to function was removed. Second, there was a "restoration" of this authority through "The Prophet," Joseph Smith.

Three levels of authority operate within Mormonism. We will focus our exploration on one – the personal level. The other two will only receive brief mention, mostly because they are dealt with elsewhere and because most authors simply don't cover this third level despite its central importance to the Mormon psyche. This third element not only creates an obstacle in sharing the gospel with Mormons, but most Christian authors spend very little time addressing it, even though it is perhaps the most germane to the approach used by the missionaries to gain converts. The first level of authority in Mormonism is the role of modern-day prophets. As is often the case, the LDS Church takes Bible verses out of context to claim that the true church must have living prophets and apostles to guide God's people. Since the death of Joseph Smith in 1844, numerous splinter groups emerged, each with its own prophetic authority figure. The major body is based in Salt Lake City, Utah, and is currently led by a living prophet. Indeed, the living prophet and his twelve apostles are the governing body the sixteen-million-member Church looks to for an authoritative voice.

The second level of authority is scripture, known collectively as the Standard Works. While Christians view Scripture as the Bible and only the Bible, LDS "scripture" includes the King James Version of the Bible, and also the Book of Mormon, the Doctrine and Covenants, and the Pearl of Great Price. While they embrace the historical sixty-six books of the Bible as authoritative, they minimize the reliability of the biblical text, and thus its authority. Joseph Smith wrote the Eighth Article of Faith, which claims that the Bible is true only as far as it is translated correctly.[5] The

---

5   Articles of Faith 8, in The Pearl of Great Price (Salt Lake City: The Church of Jesus Christ of Latter-day Saints, 2013).

implication is obvious. No matter, though, for they believe they have living prophets and other scripture.

The LDS Church believes that Smith translated the Book of Mormon – a book allegedly about the history of two people groups in the ancient Americas: the Nephites and the Lamanites. It contains the fullness of the "gospel" and describes how Jesus visited these peoples after His resurrection. Mormons claim that the Book of Mormon is another testament of Jesus Christ, whereas Christians believe it is a testament of another "Jesus Christ." The Doctrine and Covenants contains alleged revelations given to Smith, along with some others given to other latter-day prophets, but almost all prior to the twentieth century. Finally, the Pearl of Great Price contains various other books such as the books of Moses, Abraham, and a few allegedly inspired writings of Joseph Smith. Famously, it contains insight into the creation and the counsel of the gods – an allusion to polytheism, which seems inconsistent with the Book of Mormon. However, polytheism is fully consistent with Mormon teaching from Smith's late theology until present times.

The third level of authority at work in the LDS Church is personal. While this isn't an essential doctrine, it is essential to dialogue. One might expect the ultimate authority to lie with the prophet or the scriptures, but for the average Mormon, the personal testimony is ultimately authoritative. It allows for a sort of cognitive dissonance that enables them to accept contradictions in their scriptures and among their prophets while maintaining faith. This must be addressed.

The existence of all these competing authorities means that landing on a systemized theology becomes difficult – both for the Mormon and for the Christian trying to engage him. James Faulconer, the former department head of philosophy at BYU, said:

> For a Latter-day Saint, a theology is always in danger of becoming meaningless because it can always be undone by new revelation. . . . [In] speaking for God, [the Prophet] can revoke any particular belief or practice at any moment, or he can institute a new one, and he can do those things with no concern for how to make his pronouncement rationally coherent with previous pronouncements or practices.[6]

Bible-loving Christians, however, can rejoice that they have God's full and final revelation to them in His Word, which will not change. It is a firm foundation on which to build our lives and on which to invite others to do the same.

Deep Dive into the Mormon Testimony

"I bear you my testimony. I know Joseph Smith is a prophet of God! I know the Book of Mormon is the word of God. And I know that the Church of Jesus Christ of Latter-day Saints is the one true church!"

Anyone who has spoken at any length with Mormon missionaries is likely to have heard a version of this expression, which is referred to simply as "the testimony." It is often followed by a challenge to the "investigator" to pray sincerely and ask God to likewise give you a testimonial knowledge of the truth of Mormonism (based on a promise made in the Book of Mormon in Moroni 10:4). One can expect to encounter this numerous times during a discussion with missionaries.

The testimony is often delivered with such expressive tenacity that one might be tempted to conflate it with truth. At the very least, Christians are usually perplexed about how to respond.

---

6   James Faulconer, "Why a Mormon Won't Drink Coffee but Might Have a Coke: The Atheological Character of the Church of Jesus Christ of Latter-day Saints" (lecture, BYU, Provo, UT, March 19, 2003). Cited in Travis Kerns, *The Saints of Zion* (Nashville: B&H Academic, 2018), 20.

Far too many Christians walk away from spiritual conversations with Mormons deflated by the fact that Mormons seem unreceptive to all the great facts and logical arguments Christians use, but instead insist on clinging to their testimony. Despite their importance, facts don't always change minds. Instead, we need our Mormon friends to first begin to doubt their testimony before they can believe the truth we share. The best way to do this is through imaginative illustration and asking questions. After carefully and thoughtfully creating a place of doubt, we can make use of their high esteem for testimonial knowledge by deploying our own personal testimony in conjunction with the powerful objective testimony of the Bible.

Before laying out the strategic approach, we must remember a few things. First, while the Mormon approach to testimony is problematic, we do not need to discount the value of personal testimony as a legitimate form of knowledge. We use and rely on testimonial evidence quite regularly – from expert witnesses in court to asking someone for directions. There is both biblical precedent for, and rhetorical power in, sharing our own Christian testimonies. Second, as a means of locating common ground, we should initially commend (rather than attack or dismiss) the LDS members who are bearing their testimony. We can say something like, "I can see that you hold those beliefs very sincerely," or "Thank you for sharing that with me." Mentioning agreement before disagreement helps our Mormon friends to feel receptive rather than defensive. Third, we should aim to use questions and answers (rather than direct frontal assault) in order to engage, assess, and ultimately bring about psychological doubt in the Mormon's testimony. Asking thought-provoking questions helps foster reflection rather than deflection.

People are often better persuaded when they arrive at conclusions on their own instead of being directed to them by others. Most active LDS members see themselves as having the repository of religious truth. Many are former missionaries and are used to being in the role of a teacher in conversations about their faith. Let them imagine they are teaching by asking them questions, and then lead them to the truth. Fourth, given the hypnotic influence the LDS testimony has, we will make little progress in discussing other essential matters such as God and salvation if we do not first undermine confidence in their testimony.

The Bible underscores the value of testimony where properly used. God's Spirit *bears witness with our spirit that we are children of God* (Romans 8:16). In 1 John 5:9-13, the testimony of our assurance of eternal life is denoted as some sort of knowledge. Jesus says that eternal life consists in knowing God (John 17:3). Considering the Holy Spirit in the life of the New Testament believer (John 14-16), one is expected to know experientially (not merely intellectually) that God is present in and independent from the world He created. So as a Christian, it is good to feel that your faith is true, and it can be powerful to talk about your experience to others – especially when personal experience is the language Mormons understand.

The intuitive problem many people have with testimony as a form of knowledge is that it seems too subjective. If I have a testimony, and you have a different testimony, don't they cancel each other out? How can we possibly know what is true in the face of conflicting "evidence"? The problem with this objection, however, is that not all evidence is equal. Evidence needs to be weighed rather than counted. The subjective evidence must align with the objective revelation of God's Word. If a person's beliefs contradict known truths, then those beliefs would be false. Therefore, only testimonial reports that contradict truth or fail to be supportable by evidence are problematic.

Understanding the Mormon Testimony

Christians are sometimes baffled after presenting what they consider to be knockdown arguments against Mormonism, only to hear the Mormon double down about how they know it is true regardless, as if they are saying, "Never mind the facts; I've got a feeling." LDS members aspire to both gain and to "bear testimony" (i.e., a personalized, deeply felt, public declaration). They deploy it in defense when cornered, or on offense to impact an investigator.

A selection of quotes by LDS authorities helps grasp the importance of the testimony. LDS apostle Boyd K. Packer said, "A testimony is to be found in the bearing of it. Somewhere in your quest for spiritual knowledge, there is that 'leap of faith,' as the philosophers call it."[7] Surprisingly, the way for some people to discover or acquire a testimony is simply by repeating the mantra. Elsewhere, Packer reveals the nature of testimony: "Bear testimony of the things that you hope are true, as an act of faith."[8]

The Doctrine and Covenants 9:8-9 describe the testimony as a "burning in the bosom," which LDS apostle Dallin Oaks defined as "a feeling of comfort and serenity."[9] Another LDS leader encourages its use in evangelism: "Sincere feelings conveyed from heart to heart by means of testimony convert people to the truth where weak, wishy-washy, argumentative statements will not."[10] In this book, we are interacting with the official LDS Church missionary manual, called *Preach My Gospel*, which proclaims, "In order to know that the Book of Mormon is true, a person must read, ponder, and pray about it. The honest seeker of truth will soon come to feel that the

---

7   Boyd K. Packer, *That All May Be Edified* (Bookcraft, 1982), 340.

8   Packer, "The Candle of the Lord," *Ensign*, January 1983, 55.

9   Dallin Oaks, "Teaching and Learning by the Spirit," *Ensign*, March 1997, 13.

10   Gene R. Cook, "Are You a Member Missionary?" *Ensign*, May 1976, 103.

Book of Mormon is the word of God."[11] Another LDS prophet warned that failure to bear testimony frequently may result in a loss of merit points toward the heavenly goal.[12]

It appears that the more expressively the testimony is told, the truer it somehow becomes.

Paving the Way for Truth

Given the stranglehold that testimony has on Mormons, it is important to undermine confidence in it in order to open new possibilities. How do we do that?

I find it helpful to use a "police lineup" illustration. In a police lineup, the suspect of a crime stands next to several people of similar height, build, and complexion – facing the direction of the witness, who is behind a one-way mirror. The witness must identify the real culprit in contrast to the mere look-alikes, who are eliminated in the process. I begin like this:

I'm considering the testimony of Mormonism, which claims to be the true representation of God. But which Mormonism? I understand that since Joseph Smith's death, there have been and continue to be numerous competing sects to line up and examine, all of whose testimonies disagree. Only one can be right. Which church is the one true church? That is, of all those claiming to be the one true church, which is the real one true church?

Mormonism may appear uniform, but in reality, dozens of contemporary Mormon splinter groups exist. The Salt Lake City-based LDS Church is usually the one people think of when hearing the term "Mormon," but it is not alone. Most Mormons know this, even if they are unaware of just how many

---

11   *Preach My Gospel: A Guide to Missionary Service* (The Church of Jesus Christ of Latter-day Saints, 2019), 38.

12   LDS prophet Spencer W. Kimball writes, "Monthly there are testimony meetings held where each one has the opportunity to bear witness. To by-pass such opportunities is to fail to that extent to pile up credits against the accumulated errors and transgressions." See *The Miracle of Forgiveness* (Salt Lake City: Bookcraft, 1969), 205.

competing sects exist among the hundreds since its founding. Each sect is fully loaded with its own prophets and apostles claiming to hold the true "Restoration," excluding all others. Further, they all claim to have received a testimony about the truthfulness of the Book of Mormon and their authorized and restored version of Mormonism, attended with great feelings of warmth and serenity.

On venturing in this direction, the Mormon may sense a familiarity with the LDS "origin story" – when Joseph Smith went into the "Sacred Grove" to ask God which of the different Protestant churches to join. Many LDS missionaries will recount this story to people in their first missionary discussion. They often note that the multiplicity of church denominations existing today is confusing. So, they argue, we need modern revelation through a living prophet to guide us through the confusion.

The police-lineup illustration turns the tables so that it is the Mormon who is in the "Grove," so to speak, as we point out to them the diversity of their own movement and question the reliability of their testimonies over against others. It is rhetorically powerful because we are using "Mormonese" – the language of experience – and subverting their misuse of testimony while preparing to use our own testimony properly. (A Christian's testimony is likewise subjective, but corresponds to the objective testimony of Scripture, which is historically reliable.) The goal is to undermine the Mormon's confidence in their solely subjective testimony so that every time they consider bearing it in the future, they will be unable to feel confident given the residue of doubt. They will be more open to considering other things.

Here is another way to illustrate the problem with subjective testimony. Suppose that you want to ask about which of the Mormon sects you should join. You only need to name a few. The Church of Jesus Christ of Latter-day Saints (LDS) is the biggest one; others include the Fundamentalist Church of Jesus Christ of Latter-day Saints (FLDS) and the Apostolic United Brethren (AUB). Ask your friend to imagine that you gather one representative from each in a room to bear you his testimony. The Sacred Grove is recollected once again.

How might an investigator decide which of these Mormon sects is true? Logically, since each one contradicts the others, at best only one can be true and all others false. At worst, they are all false. Invoking imagination via illustration again, one could ask:

Suppose I was standing before a lineup of various sects of Mormons, each with its own set of prophets and apostles bearing testimony. How would I determine which is true? How do you know your church is true and not another? As I see it, you have a few options. Either you can judge their hearts as liars or insincere people, or you can claim that, while sincere, they are somehow deceived by a lying spirit. Which do you opt for since you must assume that your own testimony is true: are others insincere and lying, or are they sincerely deceived?

They will likely choose the latter. Continue probing.

How do you know that it is not you who are sincerely deceived in your testimony when competing Mormon sects testify of an equally strong feeling of peace and serenity? It seems to me that a subjective testimony cannot be relied upon as the sole criterion by which to determine what is true. The apostle Paul warns that it is possible to be deceived by Satan masquerading as an angel (e.g., 2 Corinthians 11:14; Galatians 1:6-9).

If Mormonism teaches a different god or a different means of salvation that contradicts the Bible, then biblical Christians should no more pray about this than pray about whether we ought to murder; God has already spoken. So, while knowledge of God can be transmitted via testimony, it is not wise to rely on subjective testimony alone, especially if our eternity hangs in the balance. Would you agree?

Sharing One's Christian Testimony

Present the gospel. Aim to communicate the essentials – such as God as holy Creator, man as sinfully separated and deserving wrath, Christ taking our punishment, and our responsibility to repent and trust in Christ's work alone to receive forgiveness.

Having planted seeds of doubt, having undermined the Mormon's testimony, and having tenaciously shared the gospel, I conclude by giving my testimony with the most explicit statement in Scripture that tests the legitimacy of a testimony. Speaking with emotional tenacity, I say, "I testify that in Jesus Christ, and Him alone, I have eternal life and will be with Heavenly Father for eternity. I'd like to share Scripture that explicitly details a true testimony that is divinely approved knowledge."

I then take them directly to 1 John 5:9-13 (NIV, emphasis added):

> *We accept human **testimony**, but God's **testimony** is greater because it is the **testimony** of God, which he has given about his Son. Whoever believes in the Son of God accepts this **testimony**. Whoever does not believe God has made him out to be a liar, because they have not believed the **testimony** God has given about his Son. And this is the **testimony**: God has given us eternal life, and this life is in his Son. Whoever has the Son has life; whoever does not have the Son of God does not have life. I write these things to you who believe in the name of the Son of God so that you may **know** that you have eternal life.*

I then ask:

Do you have this testimony? If you died today, do you know that you would experience eternal life with Heavenly Father? If not, is God a liar? I know that I have eternal life because

I trust in Christ's work alone, doing good works in grateful response to the salvation I have solely on the merits of Christ. I know this both by the Holy Spirit and by the testimony of Scripture. Mormonism does not offer the confidence that my testimony has, nor is it in harmony with God's testimony. He says that *whoever has the Son* can *know* that eternal life with their Heavenly Father is assured.

What a wonderful promise to both embrace and share!

* * * *

Corey Miller, PhD, was born in Utah as a seventh-generation Mormon. His ancestor was a polygamist and one of Joseph Smith's bodyguards. Miller is president and CEO of Ratio Christi (ratiochristi.org), a campus apologetics evangelism ministry on 150 campuses. He has four graduate degrees and has taught nearly one hundred college courses in philosophy and religion, including at Indiana and Purdue universities. He is the author of *Is Faith in God Reasonable: Debates in Philosophy, Science, and Rhetoric*; *Leaving Mormonism: Why Four Scholars Changed Their Minds*; *In Search of the Good Life: Through the Eyes of Aristotle, Maimonides, and Aquinas*; and *Engaging with Mormons*. He and his family reside in Indiana.

Chapter 3

An Insider Tour of the Missionary Experience

By Matt Wilder

Many people have died trying to climb Mount Everest. One man refused to surrender his attempt to the summit when the odds were clearly against him. Climbing at a snail's pace through the "death zone" (more than eight thousand meters in altitude) was a recipe for disaster. Every breath was a struggle as snow blindness, frostbite, exhaustion, hypothermia, and hypoxemia were settling in. This man would soon join the graveyard of frozen and exposed corpses that litter Everest's high landscape. Consumed by ambition and pride to reach the summit, he disregarded those who cautioned him to turn around, and he soon died.

The odds are impossibly against us all to ascend to heaven, God's mountaintop of eternal life, through our own efforts. I tried to work my way to God and His forgiveness through extrabiblical rules, rituals, and regulations while seeking the approval, absolution, and glory of men. This is the harsh and unforgiving mountain terrain of works-based religion, which causes exhaustion and blindness. I was gasping for the life-sustaining oxygen of God's true Word, but instead received the painful frostbite of sin's wages.

Preparing for a Mormon Mission

Serving a two-year mission was a necessary part of my LDS summit attempt. It is a command for eighteen-year-old males in the religion. President Spencer W. Kimball said in 1973, "Every boy and many girls and couples should serve missions. Every prospective missionary should prepare morally, spiritually, mentally, and financially all of his life in order to serve faithfully, efficiently, and well in the great program of missionary work."[13] For a Utah Mormon male, serving a full-time mission for the Church of Jesus Christ of Latter-day Saints is a rite of passage. Friends, family, and the local church expect him to successfully complete this two-year endeavor. To do so is a badge of honor.

After years of preparation and ecclesiastical interviews, I was considered worthy to serve a mission for the Mormon Church. During my freshman year at BYU, my mission papers (application form for missionary candidates) were sent to the Church's headquarters in Salt Lake City, Utah. The leadership there would decide where I would be serving for the next two years. I waited anxiously for months. When the official mission call came in the mail, my family gathered in celebratory fashion to see where I had been called to serve: Denmark.

LDS missionaries are the heroes of the faith, commissioned, set apart, anointed, and appointed to preach their gospel to the world. In Sunday school, children sing songs about someday joining the ranks of God's special army: "I hope they call me

---

13   Spencer W. Kimball, "Advice to a Young Man: Now Is the Time to Prepare," *New Era*, June 1973, 9.

on a mission . . ." A Mormon mission has been coined life's "best two years." Young LDS women are encouraged to marry returned missionaries who have faithfully completed this two-year service. I would now be joining God's army and reaping all its benefits.

Missionary Boot Camp

In addition to the religious and cultural expectations and pressures to go on a mission, I also had a personal zeal and sincere desire to go. I believed I would be doing God's work. But this wasn't a task to be taken lightly. LDS President Thomas S. Monson taught, "Missionary work is difficult. It taxes one's energies, it strains one's capacity, it demands one's best effort. . . . No other labor requires longer hours or greater devotion or such sacrifice and fervent prayer."[14] Serving an LDS mission is indeed no small commitment. It can require forsaking home, country, friends, family, and life as you know it to serve the Church. Those pursuing this endeavor devote two years to doctrinal study, teaching, proselytizing, serving prospective converts and the Church, and perhaps learning another language.

Missionaries going to a country where a foreign language is spoken are required to spend nine weeks at one of the missionary training hubs. The Missionary Training Center (MTC) is like a boot camp for Mormon missionaries. It is gated and has no access to the outside world. There are strict rules and an intense schedule that devours the participant's time and energy from early in the morning until late at night. There they learn the Mormon doctrine and how to teach it, as well as the language, culture, and customs of the land to which they are headed.

My nine weeks at the Provo MTC felt like an eternity. The food was mediocre at best. Something always gave us horrible

---

14   Thomas S. Monson, "That All May Hear," *Ensign*, May 1995, 49.

gas in the classroom; we suspect it was the orange juice. Learning Danish in nine weeks seemed impossible. I was restless and exhausted. We were required to wake up at 6:30 a.m., but I would get up at 5:30 a.m. to study the language. Nonstop classes and activity for nearly two months pushed my limits, and I developed a severe sinus infection with constant throbbing and barely tolerable pain.

Perhaps the headaches were just an external expression of my internal struggles that included guilt, confusion, fear, and uncertainty. I thought I was being punished and tormented for my unworthiness. Had I truly confessed every detail of my past transgressions to my bishop? When I did that stupid thing when I was sixteen, perhaps he should have given me more of a probation to earn my right back into good standing. Do I need to confess my past sins again? Maybe then all the pain (both internally and externally) would come to an end. Eventually, as the headaches subsided and the nine weeks at the MTC came to an end, I flew to Denmark to begin the next stage of my "best two years."

Overseas

As of November 2022, the Denmark Copenhagen Mission was one of 411 LDS missions.[15] These missions are geographically divided regions all over the world. Some span large areas, and some smaller, depending on the presence of the LDS Church in that part of the world. For example, the entire country of Denmark is a mission in and of itself, whereas the Florida Orlando Mission is one primarily located in central Florida.

Once in the mission field, a missionary is assigned a companion to serve in a particular area. The companionship duo

15 Scott Taylor, "Mission map: See an area-by-area breakdown of the Church's 411 missions worldwide," *Church News* online, September 30, 2022, https://www.thechurchnews.com/members/2022/9/30/23379823/map-of-lds-missions-see-area-by-area-breakdown.

will spend every waking hour together. The mission president, who presides over the mission, can at any undisclosed and uncertain time move a missionary to a new region within the given mission and reassign companionships. These blind corners – looming route detours of uncertainty on the mountain – may induce anxiety for some who prefer stability and a clear, foreknown path.

Personality quirks or conflicts among missionary pairs can magnify the stress of an already challenging situation. With limited life experience outside the home, young missionaries navigate a new world with new faces in a new land. I remember a missionary companion who was a bit of a challenge. Looking back, I realize that I was probably a poor senior companion to him. I was likely too domineering, insensitive, and impatient, and I lacked empathy. Missionaries try to learn on the fly how to cope with living and working with peers who feel like strangers at first.

At times, my climb up my mission's Everest went smoothly. I got along great with some of my companions. I remember Elder Robb, who was an odd, clumsy kid with slurred speech, thick glasses, and a voice like Eeyore.[16] He was a gentle giant of a teddy bear. He was relaxed, chill, and without trying, he was one of the funniest guys I had ever met. I enjoyed every moment with him. Missionary reassignments were sometimes a difficult and heart-wrenching transition, but sometimes they were a welcome change. Navigating the instability and everchanging mission dynamics bred stress and anxiety.

LDS missions are very structured and have hierarchical leadership. At the top of the pyramid is the mission president – typically a seasoned, lifelong, proven servant of the Church in his 60s. For a missionary's two years, he is the guide for

---

16   Male LDS missionaries are referred to as "elders" in general and by the title "Elder" for specific individuals. Female missionaries are called "sisters" in general and "Sister" for specific individuals.

traversing the mountain. At the president's right hand is the AP (Assistant to the President). Many missionaries have coveted bragging rights to this top and favored spot.

Each mission is divided into areas called zones, districts, and companionships. A zone encompasses multiple districts. Districts are composed of multiple companionship areas. Within a missionary companionship duo, one is designated the senior companion and the other the junior. A senior companion reports to his authority, a district leader. The district leaders submit to their authority, a zone leader. The zone leaders report directly to the AP, who reports to the president himself. An LDS mission is a well-oiled machine with accountability at every level, efficiently run like a business.

In my experience as an LDS missionary, an emphasis was placed on goals and numbers. There were goals for the mission as a whole, as well as goals for zones, districts, and companionships. Every day, week, and month had number goals. How many baptisms did we have this month? How many discussions did we teach today? How many invitations did we offer to investigators this week? How many new contacts did we make this afternoon? How many service opportunities did we engage in this month? The leadership pressured us to meet these goals. When we met our goals, we were praised and celebrated; when we didn't, we felt shamed, ignored, guilty, and insignificant.

LDS missionary schedules are grueling. We are up at 6:30 a.m. A typical morning would include personal LDS scripture study, prayer, language study, breakfast, and companionship study, planning, and preparation. Missionaries are expected to be out the door by 10:00 a.m. to begin proselytizing, attend appointments, and serve the community. Other than lunch and dinner, they are expected to be productive witnesses of the LDS gospel from 10:00 a.m. until 9:30 p.m. Once home for the night, missionary companionships have one hour to plan for the following day, report numbers to the authorities, and get ready for bed. Lights are out at 10:30 p.m. The only exceptions to this schedule are Sunday mornings or afternoons, when the missionaries attend their local ward (congregation), and Preparation Day. P-Day is every Monday. The morning routine remains the same. However, from 10:00 a.m. until 6:00 p.m., missionaries are permitted to shop, do laundry, write letters, and perhaps engage in a favorite hobby or sport. They are expected to begin proselytizing by 6:00 p.m. and continue until 9:30 p.m.

The demand of our missionary schedule was at times too much to handle. When I first arrived in Denmark, the companion who trained me would take a daily nap during his lunch break, even sometimes skipping lunch altogether to maximize this hour of rest. Without a car in most of my areas, we got around using public transportation. Buses and trains were always packed with people. Travel time was proselytizing time. There was nonstop pressure to be the perfectly obedient and zealous missionary.

When we lived on the edge of our missionary area, we would often stay out all day to maximize our time. We would either skip lunch or eat on the go. Dehydration and overwork led to fatigue and sickness. My mission experience ended how it started – with a miserable, head-throbbing sinus infection. I experienced daily constant headaches for months. At their peak, I could only function while sitting upright. If I tried to lay my head down, I would cross my pain threshold. Rest was fleeting, both physically and spiritually.

LDS missionaries are expected to follow a strict code of conduct. These regulations range from dress code to daily schedule routines to moral and dietary guidelines. Missionary companions must always be together within eyesight. There was no TV or movies. An avalanche of guilt or reprimand could be triggered by breaking one of the rules. When a companion breaks the rules, snitching is always a possibility. Missionaries have one-on-one interviews with the mission president and leadership on a regular basis, where issues can be addressed. A severe transgression would get a missionary kicked off his mission – a most shameful and feared possibility.

On my mission, interactions with family members and friends were limited and guarded. Mission authorities had access to our email accounts to oversee all communication. When I was an LDS missionary (2002-2004), we were only allowed to speak to family members twice a year on the phone: once on Christmas and once on Mother's Day. Isolation from family, friends, and home impacted some missionaries more than others. Homesickness and depression were common. In February 2019, the LDS Church announced an update that "missionaries may communicate with their families on their weekly preparation day via text messages, online messaging, phone calls and video chat in addition to letters and emails."[17] But in my experience of being away from home and family, ward (congregant) members became family. Strong bonds with those investigating Mormonism developed. Positive relational experiences were vital in light of the constant rejection we faced in Denmark. Some would yell disparagingly at us from afar. Others would slam doors in our faces. Most avoided us like a mouse would avoid a cat. A warm smile given, a cold beverage offered, or a lent ear could make all the difference.

Reaching LDS Missionaries

I remember a Christian family who invested in us. They were like a supply helicopter replenishing tired climbers with food cans and oxygen bottles. They genuinely loved us, took an interest in our lives, and engaged with us during our multiple

---

17   "Missionaries Now Have More Options to Communicate With Families," *Newsroom*, The Church of Jesus Christ of Latter-day Saints, February 15, 2019, https://news-room.churchofjesuschrist.org/article/missionaries-family-communication.

visits. Out of those interactions, seeds of the gospel of Jesus Christ were planted in my heart, although it would take years for them to come to fruition. The family members did more listening than speaking, but when they did share, it was impactful. Asking questions can be effective. I remember the mother of this Christian family asking us, "Why can't what Jesus did on the cross be enough for you – to save you?"

My religious summit attempt was actually a death wish. At the top of the mountain, there is not a vast river of life, a lush land of beauty, and the glory of our Creator. Rather, the summit of this works-based Everest is a rigid, narrow, icy platform surrounded by deadly cliffs, and the air is without oxygen. The wages of our vain and labor-intensive pursuit is death. Without intervention, I, too, would eventually join the masses of icy corpses on this mountain summit ridge. Who would bear me up on eagle's wings and carry me to God's holy mountain? His mountain teems with life, peace, warmth, light, and the presence of the glory of Jesus. His mountain is a land of forgiveness, rest, assurance, and eternal life.

Christians are called to the Great Commission. They are sent out to share the glory and light of Christ to a dying world. Do we look upon the works-based summit attempt of these LDS missionary kids with a broken heart of empathy and compassion? Will we watch them gasp for oxygen in this cold, barren landscape without offering a rescue to a better land and a better way?

LDS missionaries commonly struggle with issues of worthiness. When I was a missionary zone leader, I worked together with my mission president to help individuals within my zone who struggled with homesickness, depression, and issues of guilt. I was no stranger to the despair, fear, pressure, and guilt brought about in this system of perfectionism. The guilt of past sins (though previously confessed) was so overbearing that I finally hit a wall. Partway through my mission, I requested a special emergency appointment with my mission president. This disrupted his normal routine. He literally traveled across the entire country of Denmark to meet with me in person. There, in embarrassment and humiliation, I reconfessed incredibly specific details of intimate actions with my first girlfriend from four years earlier. I had already confessed those details (though more broadly) years ago to an "authority," but I still hadn't found peace. I was once again seeking absolution from a man who did not truly have the power to forgive sins. The absolution I received from my mission president would be fleeting. It was only later in life, when I sought out Jesus and cried out to Him, that I found lasting peace and forgiveness.

When witnessing to LDS missionaries, try focusing on the following points of vulnerability: worthiness, forgiveness, and assurance. Many struggle to feel worthy before God. Many have no confidence that they are forgiven or will live with God for all eternity. Many are exhausted in their effort toward perfection. Using questions to touch on these stress points can be effective. Do you ever feel unworthy? If you were to die today, where do you think you would go, and why? Are you confident that God has fully forgiven you for your sins? Do you feel you have met all your religion's requirements for eternal life?

Ultimately, we want to offer them the solution to their pain, fear, and exhaustion: the gospel of the grace of God. When I was a Mormon, I primarily viewed Jesus as my example rather than as my substitute. In other words, Jesus showed me the way to be saved, but it was up to me to follow His example and earn eternal life. But a substitute acts in our place. As our substitute, Jesus lived and died for us.

Consider a person who is in a helpless state in a deep, dark pit with no way out. The Mormon gospel would say, "Climb out." This is impossible. But the biblical gospel says, "Trust in Jesus. He will carry you out Himself and heal your wounds." This is good news! We want to communicate that we are completely forgiven and accepted by God through trusting in what Jesus has done on our behalf. He lived a perfect life and then died in our place on the cross of Calvary. Jesus took upon Himself our sin and the punishment we deserved from God for our sin. We who believe in Him have the free gift of His righteousness, forgiveness, and eternal life.

Jesus offers a better way. He says, *Come to Me, all you who labor and are heavy laden, and I will give you rest* (Matthew 11:28). Working for eternal life brings exhaustion, fear, and death. Coming to Jesus brings rest, fulfillment, contentment, and assurance. *But to him who does not work but believes on Him who justifies the ungodly, his faith is accounted for righteousness* (Romans 4:5). Our plea to the Mormon missionaries is "Come to Jesus!" He delivers from death's cold grip and breathes His warming love and life into our souls. God said to Israel, *You have seen what I did to the Egyptians, and how I bore you on eagles' wings and brought you to Myself* (Exodus 19:4). Jesus bore me on eagles' wings and brought me to Himself. He rescued me from my religious Everest and brought me to His holy mountain – a land of milk and honey with a river of life and leaves of healing for the nations. *Exalt the LORD our God, and worship at His holy hill, for the LORD our God is holy* (Psalm 99:9).

I have replaced the futile ambition of a works-based summit attempt with knowing Jesus. A personal relationship with Christ has become my fuller hope, larger dream, superior aspiration, and ultimate ambition. Jesus is the greater summit. He is rest for the weary soul. Many people are exhausted, trying to do life on their own and in their own way. They need the rest found through submission to and trust in Christ. Let's point them to Jesus.

* * * *

Matt Wilder was raised LDS and served a two-year Mormon mission in Denmark before attending BYU. There he studied piano performance for three years before leaving Mormonism. One of the founding members of Adam's Road (adamsroadministry.com) and Adam's Road Piano (adamsroadpiano.com), Matt has been involved in full-time Christian music ministry since 2006. He is also a host of the *Adam's Road* podcast (adamsroadministry.com/podcast), a weekly radio and podcast outreach. He and his family reside in Florida. He enjoys running, time with friends and family, and eating fine food.

Part 2

The LDS Missionary Discussions

Chapter 4

Missionary Lesson One: The Message of the Restoration

By Joel Fauver

Τhis book is meant to be a well-meaning and well-intentioned discussion between friends. We are assuming that the missionaries are coming to your door. These two clean-cut young men (or women) have literally given up two years of normal life to spread the news of their Church. To me, this is the hardest part of countering their message. They are sincere and true followers.

In 2002, the top leadership of the Church of Jesus Christ of Latter-day Saints said, "The day of the 'repent and go' missionary is over."[18] No more would someone be caught in serious transgression and allowed to go serve the Lord. Instead, they raised the bar. Prospective missionaries were expected to be faithful from the get-go. LDS leaders wanted young men and women who eschewed serious sins as defined by the Church,

---

18   M. Russell Ballard, "The Greatest Generation of Missionaries," *Ensign*, November 2002, 46-49.

and instead, kept themselves unspotted from the world. These young people believe the message of the restored gospel, and they are willing to give up two years of their lives to preach it. That kind of sincerity makes an armor that can seem impenetrable.

I know because I was one of these young people. My family raised me from a young age to be a faithful Latter-day Saint. I gave up credited high school courses to attend church classes on campus. I attended the mandatory three hours of church on Sundays. My father, my brothers, and I served others around us regularly. I was as dedicated to the Church as any Latter-day Saint has ever been. I was even willing to die for my faith. I gladly served a two-year, self-funded mission and thanked God for the chance to spend those two years talking to strangers about the Church. Again, this is the hardest part about talking to the missionaries. They believe thoroughly that theirs is a message of hope and salvation.

Readers of this book should remember that God draws people to Himself at His own pace and timing. He is the fisherman; we just cast the nets. He is the gardener; we just cast the seeds, water, and hope. This book does not provide a surefire way to do anything except make well-reasoned, logical arguments while appealing to Scripture. Hopefully these arguments will counter the false gospel of Mormonism in the hearts of missionaries or other Latter-day Saints you encounter.

Now that we have covered that ground, let's get down to countering the message that Latter-day Saints call the "restored gospel."

The Restored Gospel

In 2004, the leadership of the Church of Jesus Christ of Latter-day Saints, the Quorum of the Twelve Apostles, released a new book for all missionaries to teach from. It is called *Preach My*

Gospel (PMG). For years, the Church had given their emissaries standardized ways to present the message of the Church. *PMG* is intended to give missionaries a way to preach the Church's message without having to say things in a dry and clunky manner.

I happened to be at the Missionary Training Center in Provo, Utah, the very month the book was released. Our teachers at the training center were excited. They were former missionaries who volunteered time to go and teach new missionaries how to be effective. They enthusiastically explored the book with us, trying to help me and my fellow missionaries figure out dynamic and engaging ways to teach. We were videotaped as we practiced teaching so we could be coached. After two weeks of this sort of pressure cooker, we were sent into the "field," where we began to spread the "word of Jesus."

The message that we were teaching to people in this new way was that the true church organization, along with the ability to administrate in the name of God, died with the original apostles, but has been gloriously restored through the prophet Joseph Smith in the 1800s. This message, while presented in a sincere manner, means that the LDS Church firmly believes that every other believer in Christ since about 100 AD has believed in a false gospel. A verse from the Book of Mormon (their flagship revelatory text) states that there are only two churches: "The one is the church of the Lamb of God, and the other is the church of the devil" (1 Nephi 14:10). It is not hard to guess which is which.

Missionaries who come to your door or stop you in the street will begin to teach you about a loving Heavenly Father and His Son, Jesus, through whom we can be saved. This sounds very similar to Christian beliefs. Unfortunately, although it is very similar, it is also incredibly different. Their version of Jesus lived with God long ago as a spirit child. He climbed the echelons of power through His own righteousness until He attained to such a level of power and good works that He equaled the Father Himself.[19] This is according to the divine plan that the LDS prophet Joseph Smith claimed to have received through revelation. Although any missionary will balk at the idea that Jesus is a creation of the Father, it is nevertheless what their doctrine implies. They believe that all human spirits were conceived by heavenly parents before the earth was created. Jesus is included among those spirit children, undeniably making Jesus a creation. The Mormon Jesus is a creation who eventually attained the same status as the Creator.

Christian doctrine says that Jesus was with the Father from the beginning (John 1:1-3), with neither beginning of days nor end of life (Hebrews 7:3). He is someone who needs nothing to be perfected and needs no one. We need to understand this fundamental difference in beliefs. When we speak to Latter-day Saints, it is as if they are speaking a foreign language. Words mean different things to them. They say they are Christians, but they have a different Christ.

The Great Plan of Salvation

Now let's go on to the first lesson in the LDS missionary manual that missionaries tend to teach: the restoration of the gospel of Jesus Christ. In my missionary notes, when I created my lesson plans, I somewhat jokingly called this lesson, "It's Back!!!" I was very confident that this was the most important thing for anyone whom I met to hear.

In LDS doctrine, the Father planned to send His numberless spirit children to earth to inhabit earthly bodies so they could become gods, just like He had done. His plan was for these spirit children to be born on earth, where they would forget their time in heaven and be tested to see if they would choose

---

19   Abraham 3:22-27 (Pearl of Great Price).

to be faithful. If they would follow the doctrine laid out by the Church of Jesus Christ, and if they would do the works they were told to do, then they would rise to heaven to become like God in every respect. This includes going so far as having their own spiritual children who could one day go on to inhabit a planet much like ours.

Patterns of Apostasy

The LDS Church wants us to believe that God has always called a prophet to lead His church. They will tell you that people such as Adam and Noah administered a church – even though this is never spoken of in the Bible. These prophets also supposedly included Melchizedek, Seth, Abraham, and others. Each prophet is said to have had a unique message for the children of God. They say that God sends these messengers out of love for His children whom He is trying to bring to Himself. This point is belabored quite often in LDS doctrine. The missionaries want you to buy into the idea that prophets have a modern-day iteration because they are crucial and necessary for God's plan to succeed. Their entire religion stands or falls on the idea that modern-day revelators exist.

The truth is that there are sometimes gaps of hundreds of years between prophets mentioned in the Bible. There is no biblical record of any prophets beyond the ones we have in the text. Most importantly, Hebrews 1:1-2 speaks very eloquently and succinctly about the existence of prophets, as well as the termination of the prophetic word after the coming of Jesus. Jesus is our High Priest. Jesus is our Prophet, the messenger of God sent to advocate for us. All prophets were signs pointing to Jesus. Now that He has come, we no longer need prophets who point us to God. God Himself came to lead us.

Lesson one in the LDS manual attempts to establish the belief that prophetic dispensations exist. Because God is the same yesterday, today, and forever, *surely the Lord God does nothing, unless He reveals His secret to His servants the prophets* (Amos 3:7). In response, we must emphasize the point that all history turned on the crux of our Savior, Jesus, and His death. Prophets before spoke of His coming, but after He was raised from the dead, He had no more need for prophets to prophesy of His pending birth. He had been born. His work is completed. We are now awaiting His return.

When Jesus was on earth, He was the ultimate prophet. LDS missionaries will concede this point. Anything you would expect from a prophet, our Lord was – and more. With His death and resurrection, He ushered in a new age of belief where daily intercession in a temple was no longer needed. No priests are necessary. No offerings are required beyond a broken heart and contrite spirit (Psalm 51:17; Hebrews 4:14-16; Hebrews 5-10). They will agree with this narrative – with one caveat. Missionaries will say that while Jesus was here, He gave special representatives, known as apostles, special authority to act for Him through the laying on of His hands (John 15:16). They will try to establish that this authority was required for the apostles to administrate the new church, to perform miracles, and to give others the sacred rites of the faith. These rites include baptism, laying on of hands for the Holy Spirit, priesthood ordination, marriage, blessing of the sick, and many others. This assumption is based on passages in the New Testament that show Jesus or an apostle laying their hands on someone and then something happening, such as the Holy Spirit falling on them (Acts 19:6) or they being healed (Acts 28:8). Nothing of a spiritual nature is done in the LDS Church without authorization from those in authority, yet the book of Hebrews counters this approach:

> *For you have not come to the mountain that may be*
> *touched and that burned with fire, and to blackness*

*and darkness and tempest, and the sound of a trum-
pet and the voice of words, so that those who heard
it begged that the word should not be spoken to
them anymore. (For they could not endure what was
commanded: "And if so much as a beast touches the
mountain, it shall be stoned or shot with an arrow."
So terrifying was the sight that Moses said, "I am
exceedingly afraid and trembling.")*

*But you have come to Mount Zion and to the city of
the living God, the heavenly Jerusalem, to an innu-
merable company of angels, to the general assembly
and church of the firstborn who are registered in
heaven, to God the Judge of all, to the spirits of just
men made perfect, to Jesus the Mediator of a new
covenant, and to the blood of sprinkling that speaks
better than that of Abel.* (Hebrews 12:18-24)

The problem is that relying on authoritative prophetic leaders
like Moses brings us back under the Old Testament. Many other
churches besides the LDS Church have fallen into this trap.

Moving on, LDS doctrine states that like the prophets of every
dispensation, the apostles were rejected. This time, though, the
most important part to this message – the authority to act for
God – was lost with the apostles' deaths. What follows in the LDS
narrative is a dark and godless age where no one could properly
discern what parts of the Bible were true. The LDS Church teaches
that pernicious priests modified manuscripts to distort the pure
message of Christ into something that fit their own ends. The
world supposedly languished in this darkness until God saw fit
to send His Spirit again to the earth to move among mankind.

Many Latter-day Saints believe that this began with the
Renaissance. During the Crusades and Dark Ages, God was

content to wait silently for humanity to be ready. The Renaissance is seen by them as the first evidence that God was moving again among mankind. Scientific and religious ideas were flowering. Challenges to the Catholic Church and its dogma were taken more seriously by large swaths of people, and for the first time in its long history, the Catholic Church had dissenters who eventually formed their own sects. The growing use of the printing press sped the blooming of knowledge and thought that the Catholic Church had long repressed.

We need to understand a few things about the LDS narrative at this point. Even though LDS missionaries claim that there has been a total apostasy or falling away (1 Timothy 4:1-3), this claim relies on a faulty interpretation of Scripture. They also have no evidence that any loss of doctrinal cohesion or any loss of spiritual authority as exercised by a professing believer occurred.

It is assumed by the LDS Church that authority to perform these spiritual acts ceased to exist with the death of the apostles. In his book *Jesus the Christ*, LDS scholar James E. Talmage goes into depth about how there was a cessation of apostolic authority. The Latter-day Saints rely on interpretations of Scripture from the King James Version of the Bible to make their claims. Since all authority is considered lost, the Latter-day Saints make it a point to discredit the veracity of the Bible.

They do not believe that the Bible alone is God's Word. They believe that the Bible as we know it was corrupted through a sort of long scheme carried out by the devil. Without prophetic authority to interpret Scripture, it was left up to the best efforts of man, who, as we know, is corruptible. Again, without evidence, LDS scholars contend that well-meaning scribes, or perhaps others under the influence of Satan, made changes to the Bible. These LDS scholars will tell you that with so many errors in transmission over such a long time, the inevitable conclusion is that the Bible cannot be trusted to convey the true message of salvation.

Yet a look at the staggering number of biblical manuscripts available today refutes this idea. The science of textual criticism uses the wealth of more than twenty thousand New Testament manuscripts to provide us with a virtual reconstruction of the original. Despite minor differences, the truth is that there was no substantial corruption of the Word of God.

Understand what the LDS missionaries are trying to accomplish. Like some lawyers, they do a great job of setting up a believable narrative while hiding behind the shadows of what is possible versus what is actually verifiable. They gloss over large periods of time and an array of facts that don't fit their narrative. They believe in a chain of Old Testament prophets who always received priestly authority, always taught of a coming Messiah, and were always rejected. Jesus Himself follows this pattern, as well as the apostles. Then comes the long night – the sad but inevitable consequence of rejecting the Son of God: a spiritual darkness ensued that lasted a millennium or more.

As you listen to a Mormon friend, or missionaries who come to your home, they will build a case that leads toward the Great Restoration. Mormons see their message and their faith as the true message of salvation for the world. The favorite example missionaries used to use (including me) was that of a car. Imagine the church of Christ as a classic car. (As with any metaphor, if stretched too far, it loses its usefulness.) God wants His classic car restored. The car started out very elegant and beautiful, but it has suffered because of the ravages of time, well-meaning but misguided mechanics, and perhaps even treachery. Sadly, this once beautiful automobile is only a shadow of its former glory. It is unable to run or to provide conveyance anywhere! When this car is found by a person who loves it and desires to restore it, imagine what practical steps its owner would take. Would the owner want parts manufactured this year? No! They would want original parts that had been manufactured at the same time the car was in use and that matched the car itself. Paint would be applied, upholstery redone, and glass replaced. The loving owner would do everything in his power to restore his beloved car to its original condition.

The LDS Church claims that this is exactly what happened. In 1820, Joseph Smith, a sincere young farm boy, sought the truth amid a flurry of religious revival. He wanted to know what was true. Were any of these myriad churches the single vehicle that God was using to bring salvation to mankind? He read the Bible. He sought help from ministers and religious friends.

Listen to Smith describe his experience in his own words:

> My mind at times was greatly excited, the cry and tumult were so great and incessant. The Presbyterians were most decided against the Baptists and Methodists and used all the powers of both reason and sophistry to prove their errors, or, at least, to make the people think they were in error. On the other hand, the Baptists and Methodists in their turn were equally zealous in endeavoring to establish their own tenets and disprove all others.

> In the midst of this war of words and tumult of opinions, I often said to myself: What is to be done? Who of all these parties are right; or, are they all wrong together? If any one of them be right, which is it, and how shall I know it?

> While I was laboring under the extreme difficulties caused by the contests of these parties of religionists, I was one day reading the Epistle of James, first chapter and fifth verse, which reads: *If any of you lack wisdom, let him ask of God, that giveth to all men liberally, and upbraideth not; and it shall be given him.*

Never did any passage of Scripture come with
more power to the heart of man than this did at
this time to mine. It seemed to enter with great
force into every feeling of my heart. I reflected
on it again and again, knowing that if any person
needed wisdom from God, I did; for how to act I
did not know, and unless I could get more wisdom
than I then had, I would never know; for the teachers of religion of the different sects understood
the same passages of scripture so differently as to
destroy all confidence in settling the question by
an appeal to the Bible.

At length I came to the conclusion that I must
either remain in darkness and confusion, or else I
must do as James directs, that is, ask of God. I at
length came to the determination to "ask of God,"
concluding that if he gave wisdom to them that
lacked wisdom, and would give liberally, and not
upbraid, I might venture.

So, in accordance with this, my determination
to ask of God, I retired to the woods to make the
attempt. It was on the morning of a beautiful, clear
day, early in the spring of eighteen hundred and
twenty. It was the first time in my life that I had
made such an attempt, for amidst all my anxiet-
ies I had never as yet made the attempt to pray
vocally. After I had retired to the place where I had
previously designed to go, having looked around
me, and finding myself alone, I kneeled down and
began to offer up the desires of my heart to God.
I had scarcely done so, when immediately I was

seized upon by some power which entirely overcame me, and had such an astonishing influence
over me as to bind my tongue so that I could not
speak. Thick darkness gathered around me, and
it seemed to me for a time as if I were doomed to
sudden destruction.

But, exerting all my powers to call upon God to
deliver me out of the power of this enemy which had
seized upon me, and at the very moment when I was
ready to sink into despair and abandon myself to
destruction – not to an imaginary ruin, but to the
power of some actual being from the unseen world,
who had such marvelous power as I had never
before felt in any being – just at this moment of great
alarm, I saw a pillar of light exactly over my head,
above the brightness of the sun, which descended
gradually until it fell upon me.

It no sooner appeared than I found myself delivered from the enemy which held me bound. When
the light rested upon me I saw two Personages,
whose brightness and glory defy all description,
standing above me in the air. One of them spake
unto me, calling me by name and said, pointing to
the other – "This is My Beloved Son. Hear Him!"

My object in going to inquire of the Lord was to
know which of all the sects was right, that I might
know which to join. No sooner, therefore, did I
get possession of myself, so as to be able to speak,
than I asked the Personages who stood above me
in the light, which of all the sects was right (for at

this time it had never entered into my heart that all were wrong) – and which I should join.

I was answered that I must join none of them, for they were all wrong; and the Personage who addressed me said that all their creeds were an abomination in his sight; that those professors were all corrupt; that: "they draw near to me with their lips, but their hearts are far from me, they teach for doctrines the commandments of men, having a form of godliness, but they deny the power thereof."[20]

This is the beginning of what the Mormon story refers to as the Restoration (a much more radical concept than the Reformation). God's church, lost to time through the corruption of mankind, was brought back through a sincere but flawed messenger named Joseph Smith. No attacks will be made here on Smith's character, but to any well-meaning inquirer, the claims the LDS Church makes about Joseph Smith should be taken cautiously and examined carefully. The Mormon narrative will tell you that Smith began the arduous journey of restoring the church of God, that he was led to translate the Book of Mormon by the power of God, and that this finally cleared up all the confusion created by Satan's corruption of the Bible.

They claim that Joseph Smith was visited by John the Baptist, Peter, James and John, Isaiah, Moses, and even Jesus Himself. All the prophets of past ages visited the prophet Joseph to restore the knowledge and priesthood powers that had been lost through time. All past ages converged through the twenty or more years Joseph Smith was prophet to create the Church of Jesus Christ of Latter-day Saints. This, he claimed,

---

20   Joseph Smith: History 9-19 (Pearl of Great Price).

was a restoration of the original church that Jesus established while He was here. This church was complete with baptisms for the dead, regimented priestly roles, temples (where people must prove their worthiness to enter and receive sacred/secret knowledge to gain salvation), and much more.

If you pause here and take note that none of those things were part of the original church of Jesus Christ, you would be correct. Latter-day Saints, though, are proud of these features because they say that they reflect their open canon and the church's ongoing restoration. They believe that even more is to come.

This is the conclusion that all the missionaries are building toward from the beginning of Lesson 1. They will tell you sincerely that they know, by the power of the Holy Spirit, that Joseph Smith is a prophet. I have done the very same thing. I sat with youth ministers, pastors, parishioners, and everyone in between, and told them that I knew that Joseph Smith was a real prophet. Unfortunately, as sincere as they are, this message and these kinds of prophets run counter to the Bible.

In 2017, I had a crisis of faith. God began drawing me to Himself. I looked to the LDS Church to shore up my failing faith, and I received no help. When Latter-day Saints are confronted with the simple truth of the gospel of Jesus Christ and the fallacy of all the extrabiblical teachings of the Latter-day Saints, the hardest challenge for them is not that they might lose their faith, but that they will lose their support system, their community, and their salvation.

We must remember this. To them, there are only two churches. In sharing the truth of Christ, we confront them with the idea that the gospel is simpler than they ever believed, and the organization that gave them the life they have is based on false ideas.

I faced this challenge in the fall of 2017, and I chose to follow the Bible. I rejected my false faith. I embraced the truth that Jesus's death and resurrection was what saved me. I realized that I only needed one Prophet, Priest, and King, and only one Mediator between God and man: Jesus Christ (1 Timothy 2:5). The priesthood that Jesus has lasts forever.

We were rejected by our community, we have lost friends, and our family did not understand the change in our values and beliefs. Yet the struggle has been worth it, for we have gained Jesus. We have confidence in our eternal destiny because we trust in Christ.

* * * *

Joel Fauver grew up in Idaho Falls, Idaho, and was raised as a Latter-day Saint. He served a two-year mission in the Raleigh, North Carolina Mission from 2004 to 2006. Joel is a fifth-generation Mormon, with relatives who came across the plains with the pioneers and helped settle Utah. After returning home, Joel met and married his wife in the Mesa, Arizona Temple in 2008. After leaving the church in 2017, he sought a place to share his experience of finding the grace of Jesus Christ outside of Mormonism. He enjoys swimming, watching movies, and spending time with his wife and four children.

Chapter 5

Missionary Lesson Two: The Plan of Salvation

By Matthew D. Eklund

Involvement in the Church of Jesus Christ of Latter-day Saints (or LDS Church) was the norm for those who, like me, grew up in northern Utah. Though I attended Sunday School, sacrament meetings, and Primary somewhat regularly as a child, I never felt pressured by my parents to join the Church, and it wasn't a topic that came up frequently during conversation. Reaching and passing the age of eight years old, when most LDS kids were baptized, I had not yet been baptized. I began wondering if I could enter heaven without baptism. With the goal of being baptized and joining the Church, I asked my parents to receive the LDS missionary lessons. When I was ten years old, I was baptized by my uncle on the same day as my eight-year-old sister. It was a special day for me, even though at the time I didn't understand the responsibilities I would be taking on.

In the following years, my parents divorced, and I gradually lost interest in God and religion. However, when I began attending college, several events occurred that convicted me for my past mistakes. I was always a perfectionist, and these events made me realize I wasn't a good person at heart and needed to change. After investigating different religions and feeling that the LDS Church was still the most logical choice, I began to seriously study the Book of Mormon and other books of LDS scripture. After nearly two years of study and preparation, I felt I had received a strong spiritual witness of the truthfulness of the Book of Mormon. This witness served as a personal sign of the necessity of the restoration of Christ's church through the prophet Joseph Smith, and a sign of the necessity for modern prophets. While seeking this witness, I determined that if I were to finally receive it, I would serve a mission. After being convinced that I had received this witness, I submitted my paperwork several months later to apply to become a missionary. Two weeks later, I received the call to serve in the Belgium-Brussels/Netherlands mission and to enter the Missionary Training Center in August 2007. Though my mission was long and difficult, I enjoyed the experience and strived to work as hard as I could to bring others to Christ.

In the summer of 2008, I was stationed in the city of Amiens, France, as a senior companion. This was the third area in which I had served after having been in the mission field for nearly a year. On an otherwise normal, uneventful day, with hours set aside to contact people on the streets, we encountered a young woman in her mid-20s. Instead of following the usual street-contacting routine, I had the idea of being more forward. I approached her on the sidewalk as boldly, yet also as politely, as I could to ask, "Excuse me. Did you know that you're a child of God?" The woman stopped dead in her tracks and was visibly quite taken aback at this statement. That simple but provocative statement was enough to engage her in a conversation.

The message that all humans are children of God is shared by more than fifty thousand young LDS missionaries every year with people all over the world. But why is this so important and unique? Does it conform to what the Bible says? Let's examine what the LDS Church calls the "Plan of Salvation." This is the second missionary lesson in the *Preach My Gospel* manual. It is my goal to give the basics of this lesson to prepare you for a meeting with the missionaries.

Life before Birth – The Premortal World

While Lesson 1 is setting the stage for why the world should join the LDS Church, Lesson 2 is designed to demonstrate to you the reason why *you* should join the LDS Church. It attempts to tackle the looming questions of our existence that have baffled even the most brilliant philosophers of the ages: "Where did we come from?" "Why are we here?" "Where do we go after we die?" At some point in life, everyone has asked themselves these questions, and the LDS missionary claims to have the answers to all of them.

Lesson 1 opens with the phrase, "God is our Heavenly Father," but the lesson does not give much detail as to *how* he is our "Heavenly Father."[21] Lesson 2 backfills this statement with further teachings about who God is and how we relate to Him:

> God is the Father of our spirits. We are literally His children, and He loves us. We lived as spirit children of our Father in Heaven before we were born on this earth. We were not, however, like our Heavenly Father, nor could we ever become like Him and enjoy all the blessings that He enjoys without the experience of living in mortality with a physical body.[22]

---

21 *Preach My Gospel*, 31.
22 *Preach My Gospel*, 48.

We learn several key things here. First, prior to coming to earth, all humanity supposedly lived in the existence of God, the Creator of our universe. Second, not only did we live with God, but He was *literally* our father (though of our spirits, since we did not yet have physical bodies). The LDS Church also affirms that we have a Heavenly Mother: "Each is a beloved spirit son or daughter of heavenly parents, and, as such, each has a divine nature and destiny."[23] Third, the passage explains that although we were in the presence of God and were without sin or sorrow, we were still found to be lacking something. We were not yet in a complete state of happiness. We were God's literal children, and He wanted more for us. He wanted us to have a physical body like He has and to enjoy the kind of life He lives.

The LDS missionary will describe how Heavenly Father devised a plan whereby all of His children may become like Him and have a similar level of happiness and existence. Heavenly Father's plan promised that those who would accept His plan would come to earth, receive a physical body, and would have the possibility (although not the surety) of becoming like He is and to enjoy all His blessings. In God's plan, the sojourn on earth would be a time of testing and trial. We would be tested in regard to whether we would follow good or evil. Sin would also exist, and overcoming sin would require a Savior to atone for mankind and provide a way to be free from the consequences of these sins – namely, death and separation from God's presence. Jesus was chosen in the premortal council in heaven to come to earth as mankind's Savior. Those who follow the laws and ordinances of the gospel would be able to return to live with Heavenly Father after this life. This is the gospel, the "good news," as taught in greater detail in *PMG* Lesson 3, titled "The Gospel of Jesus Christ."

---

23   The First Presidency and Council of the Twelve Apostles of the Church of Jesus Christ of Latter-day Saints, "The Family: A Proclamation to the World," September 23, 1995, https://www.churchofjesu-schrist.org/study/scriptures/the-family-a-proclamation-to-the-world/the-family-a-proclamation-to-the-world?lang=eng.

Since trials and testing require opposition, the opposing force to God in this "Plan of Salvation" is the great deceiver, the devil, whom the Latter-day Saints believe was also a literal child of God, just as we are. This makes the devil our literal spirit brother, just as Jesus and all of humanity are spirit brothers and sisters. Despite being subjected to the temptations from the devil, God promised His children that they would be agents unto themselves to choose their own destinies. "Agency, or the ability to choose, is one of God's greatest gifts to His children. Our eternal progression depends on how we use this gift. We must choose whether to follow Jesus Christ or follow Satan."[24] Those who choose to follow God's plan will be blessed and return to live with Him, while those who reject this plan will forfeit such blessings.

This plan of progression required a place where mankind could receive bodies and be tested. This leads to the next topic: the creation.

In the Beginning, the Gods . . .

While the LDS Church believes in the biblical creation account, the Book of Abraham (a book of LDS scripture) says that it wasn't as simple as *In the beginning God created the heavens and the earth* (Genesis 1:1). Instead, the Book of Abraham states: "And the Lord said: Let us go down. And they went down at the beginning, and they, that is the Gods, organized and formed the heavens and the earth."[25] The "Gods" have been variously understood to be the Father and Jesus, who are separate gods, and possibly including a council of other exalted beings. What the Latter-day Saint does agree upon is that this world was created by Jesus Christ under the direction of Heavenly Father.

---

24   *Preach My Gospel*, 48.
25   Book of Abraham 4:1 (Pearl of Great Price).

Regarding the manner of creation, Abraham describes the heavens and the earth as being "organized" and "formed" instead of "created." This is because Joseph Smith taught that God is incapable of creating matter out of nothing.[26] Instead, the Latter-day Saints believe that preexistent chaotic matter was organized into the world in which we live.

Now that the play is written and the stage is set, the actors of this drama, our first parents, must be introduced into the first scene.

The Rise of Adam and Eve

Before all humanity could come to earth, God chose to create the first man, Adam, out of the dust of the earth. Adam, who is designated as the archangel Michael, was the first spirit child of Heavenly Father who was chosen to receive a physical body on earth.[27] He was created in "the image of God," a phrase that the Latter-day Saints interpret to be physical and literal. Adam was, in essence, a carbon copy of God the Father, albeit with a body that was not in a glorified, exalted state. In the beginning, Adam was created without the negative effects of aging, sickness, or death. Eve was created to be for Adam *a helper comparable to him* (Genesis 2:18, 20). They were placed in the garden of Eden, where they lived in a paradise without evil or sin and where all their needs were taken care of. All that God required of Adam and Eve was to take care of the garden and to keep the commandments that He would give to them.

Two important commandments were given to Adam and Eve while in the garden. First, they were commanded to procreate and have children to fill the earth so that all of God's

---

26   Joseph Smith, "Discourse, 7 April 1844, as published in Times and Seasons," The Joseph Smith Papers, 615, accessed November 17, 2022, https://www.josephsmithpapers.org/paper-summary/discourse-7-april-1844-as-reported-by-times-and-seasons/4.

27   See Doctrine and Covenants 27:11; 107:53-57; 128:21.

children in the premortal world could receive physical bodies. Second, they were told that they could eat from every tree in the garden except from the *tree of the knowledge of good and evil* (Genesis 2:17). They were forbidden to eat from this tree, but they were still given the ability to choose whether to eat from this tree or not. If they kept the command to abstain from eating from that tree, they would be able to stay in the garden indefinitely in their original state of sinlessness. However, if they did this, they would remain innocent in their knowledge of procreation and would therefore be ignorant of or incapable of having children.[28]

The bride and groom were in a predicament: if they obeyed God by refusing to eat from the tree of the knowledge of good and evil, they would remain in a state of innocence and would have no children, disobeying God's command to fill the earth with offspring. If they disobeyed and ate the forbidden fruit, they would gain the knowledge for procreation, allowing them to obey the second command. They were placed in a situation in which it was impossible for them to be obedient to both commandments simultaneously; they were only capable of keeping one commandment or the other, but not both.

God declared that if they disobeyed the command to not eat the forbidden fruit, they would die. However, they would not altogether immediately die, but they would gradually die physically (by becoming mortal and being subject to age, sickness, and physical death) and immediately die spiritually (by being removed from the presence of God, which they had enjoyed up to that point).

Adam and Eve, being tempted by Satan, disobeyed God and took the forbidden fruit. They were then cast out of paradise and subjected to the pains, sicknesses, and death of mortality. However, this is seen as a positive development since it allowed

---

28   2 Nephi 2:22-23 (Book of Mormon).

for the rest of God's children to come to earth, and it allowed them to experience true joy and happiness in opposition to sorrow. This is why the "fall" of Adam and Eve from the LDS perspective can be considered to be a rise or progression in God's plan. Their action can be summed up by a single verse in the Book of Mormon: "Adam fell that men might be, and men are that they might have joy."[29]

As Adam and Eve did not yet have a full knowledge of good and evil, the Latter-day Saints do not refer to this event of taking the forbidden fruit as a "sin," but instead as a "transgression." They were not fully conscious of the wrongfulness of their actions and were thus not held fully accountable.

Life on Earth

Those who chose in the premortal world to follow God's plan were allowed to progress to the mortal world by being born in physical bodies. In so doing, we went through the "veil of forgetfulness" whereby our knowledge, memories, and experiences of living in God's direct presence were forgotten. This forces us to choose right and wrong and to "walk by faith rather than by sight"; otherwise, we couldn't be properly tested for our faithfulness.[30] In every choice we make, we use our ability to choose good or evil, righteousness or sin, and we are capable of choosing good just as we are capable of committing evil.

When we came to earth at birth, our spirit bodies were clothed in physical bodies like God's. However, ours differ from God's because of the fall; we are not yet perfected, immortal, or glorified like Heavenly Father is, so we must live in this life subject to sickness, pain, and death. We are also subject to yielding to temptations, both external and internal, physical and spiritual, and are able to commit sin, which is the breaking

---

29   2 Nephi 2:25 (Book of Mormon).
30   *Preach My Gospel*, 48.

of God's commandments. LDS members focus on how sin is unhappiness and righteousness is happiness. The "Plan of Salvation" is often called the "plan of happiness," whereby if they live according to all the "laws and ordinances of the gospel," they will receive forgiveness of sins, they will be able to return to live with Him, and they will be happy.[31] This entire plan is God's "work and [His] glory – to bring to pass the immortality and eternal life of man."[32]

At the center of this plan is Jesus Christ, the literal Son of God who was chosen in the premortal council to be our Savior. Christ came to earth, lived out His Father's plan and commandments perfectly, and suffered for our sins so that we can have eternal life if we follow God's plan. The next section tells in greater detail about Christ's atonement.

The Universal Atonement: From the Garden to the Tomb

After Christ volunteered to be the Savior of humanity, it was decided that He would be born of the virgin Mary by means of a miraculous intervention from God. Christ was literally the Son of God according to both His spirit and His physical body, whereas the rest of God's children are only His children according to the spirit. Being both the literal son of God and the firstborn spirit son of God the Father and God the Mother, Christ was enabled to live as a mortal while remaining completely without sin.

It is Jesus's sinless nature that qualified Him to be the Savior of humanity. Only the spotless Lamb of God could atone for the sins of humanity. Not only did the atonement have to be accomplished by one who was completely without sin, but the atonement also had to be infinite (without bounds in terms of

31   *Preach My Gospel*, 58.
32   Moses 1:39 (Pearl of Great Price).

efficacy or power regarding to whom and for how many sins it can be applied) and eternal (without limitations in terms of time).[33] Unlike the Old Testament animal sacrifices in the tabernacle and temple that had to be performed regularly every single year, Jesus's sacrifice was once for all time.

Jesus accomplished the atonement over the course of multiple days. It began in the garden of Gethsemane the night He was betrayed by Judas, continued the next day when He died on the cross, and was completed on the day that He rose from the dead.

In the garden of Gethsemane, Jesus took upon Him the sins of all mankind and suffered so greatly that He bled from every pore in His body.[34] Jesus overcame physical death by suffering and dying on the cross at Calvary and by rising from the grave. When Jesus died, His spirit separated from His body, at which time He went to the spirit world. On the third day after His death, Jesus was resurrected when His spirit reunited with His body. His resurrected body had been rejuvenated and perfected into a glorified state just like His Father's body. Jesus's resurrection grants every human being everywhere, whether good or evil, the gift of resurrection. That is why this aspect of the atonement is unconditional (meaning we don't have to do anything to receive it) and unlimited (everyone will receive it). Passages in the Bible that speak of salvation as a free gift, such as Ephesians 2:8-9, are sometimes described by LDS missionaries as speaking specifically of the resurrection since it is a completely free gift given to all, whereas exaltation and eternal life are not completely free gifts, but have conditions attached to them.

The Book of Mormon describes Jesus's victory over physical death, stating that in addition to "loos[ing] the bands of death," Jesus took upon Himself "the pains and the sicknesses of his people."[35] In this sense, the Latter-day Saints look toward the

---

33   See Alma 34:9-14 (Book of Mormon).
34   See Mosiah 3:7-8 (Book of Mormon).
35   Alma 7:11-13 (Book of Mormon).

atonement not only as the source for forgiveness of sins, but also for comfort in trials, sicknesses, and suffering. Every possible negative state of the human condition was felt by Jesus in the garden of Gethsemane and on the cross. In this way, He can "succor his people according to their infirmities" as they draw closer to God.[36]

Since "the Lord cannot look upon sin with the least degree of allowance,"[37] Christ's atonement was provided so that we can become completely clean of our sins. If we choose to follow the laws and ordinances of the gospel and walk the path that God has given us in the Plan of Salvation, we can receive the benefits of Jesus's atonement through faith in Jesus Christ, repentance from sin, receiving baptism and the gift of the Holy Spirit, taking the sacrament every week (bread and water – what most Christians call the Eucharist or the Lord's Supper), and enduring to the end. This is described in more detail in *PMG* Chapters 3 and 4. As we follow Christ, strive to live the commandments, and "do all things whatsoever the Lord [our] God shall command [us]," we will continue to receive forgiveness of sins and become more like Christ.[38]

When we are brought before Christ to be judged after death, we will be punished or rewarded in the afterlife based on whether we accepted the gospel and how faithful we were to our covenants made in baptism and other ordinances. But before we stand before God to be judged and sorted into a final resting place in the eternities, the spirit world awaits us.

The Spirit World

Upon death, our spirits leave our physical bodies to enter the spirit world, where we retain our personalities, knowledge, and behavior from mortality. Those who knowingly chose

---

36   Alma 7:12 (Book of Mormon).

37   See Alma 45:16 (Book of Mormon) and Doctrine and Covenants 1:31.

38   Abraham 3:25 (Pearl of Great Price).

to reject Christ on earth will still reject Him, and those who loved Christ will still love Him. We will still require spiritual and intellectual growth and progression, which implies that we will possibly still sin in the spirit world. However, there will be the continuing availability to practice repentance for the forgiveness of sins.

In the spirit world, there is a division between the righteous (those who believe and follow Christ) and the wicked (those who don't believe in or follow Christ) by being separated into "paradise" and "spirit prison." The Book of Mormon describes that we will remain in our respective domains, whether in a "state of happiness . . . rest . . . peace" or in a "state of awful, fearful looking for the . . . wrath of God upon [us]" in the spirit world until the resurrection.[39] At the resurrection, the spirits of every human who lived on earth will be reunited with their physical bodies in a complete and immortal state.

According to LDS teaching, missionary work, along with spiritual growth and repentance, is being performed in the spirit world (much like how it is done on earth right now). Upon Christ's death, He also entered the spirit world and prepared faithful servants who were waiting in paradise to share the gospel with those who had not heard the good news of the gospel.[40] The two biblical texts used to support the doctrine that Jesus shared the gospel in the spirit world are 1 Peter 3:18-20 and 1 Peter 4:6. Those who accept the LDS gospel in the spirit world and receive the essential ordinances that are performed in the LDS temples on their behalf will pass from spirit prison to paradise. This reveals the reason their temple ceremonies are so special to them: both they and their deceased ancestors are prepared by these ceremonies to enter God's presence as families knit together by the priesthood. This will be described in greater detail in *PMG* Lesson 5, "Laws and Ordinances."

---

39   Alma 40:12-14 (Book of Mormon).
40   See Doctrine and Covenants 138.

Resurrection, Judgment, and Mansions in Heaven

While resurrection is given to all, "eternal life and exaltation are gifts of God given to those who fully obey the gospel of Jesus Christ."[41] After every soul has had the opportunity to hear and accept or reject the gospel and has been resurrected, whether righteous or wicked, they must stand before Christ to be judged. The judgment is when we are sorted into our final resting places; it is the point of no return. There is no reset button or second chance once we stand before God to be judged. The Bible describes the "books" being opened by which we will be judged at the last day (Revelation 20:12). If we have accepted Christ in faith, repented of our sins, received the saving priesthood ordinances, and endured to the end by obeying God and keeping all of our covenants, we will return to live with Heavenly Father. Otherwise, we will still have the shame and guilt of our sins upon us and will not receive all of the blessings God has in store for the faithful.

Jesus told His disciples, *In My Father's house are many mansions* (John 14:2). LDS members see this in a more literal fashion in that there are separations within heaven, and which one they go to depends on their faithfulness. Those who accepted the gospel and the saving ordinances of baptism and the gift of the Holy Spirit by priesthood holders within the LDS Church (whether in life or from those who performed the ordinances by proxy in an LDS temple) and endured faithfully to the end will be sorted into the highest kingdom of glory – the celestial kingdom.

Within the celestial kingdom itself, there are three separations. The highest step is that of the status of exaltation. That is where the LDS members who keep all their covenants made in baptism receive the priesthood (for men), and those who remain faithful in their temples will remain sealed to their spouse (or spouses, as men can be sealed to more than one woman in the LDS temple

---

41   *Preach My Gospel*, 58.

in their lifetime and potentially remain sealed to them) and their children in heaven. They will become just as Heavenly Father is now with the promise that "They shall pass by the angels, and the gods, which are set there, to their exaltation and glory in all things. . . . Then shall they be gods, because they have no end; therefore, they shall be from everlasting to everlasting."[42] Receiving exaltation (also called eternal life, or "eternal lives") is the highest goal of every LDS member, and it is the goal of missionaries to prepare other people to receive that same glory.[43]

The second kingdom, the terrestrial kingdom, is prepared for those who stand at the judgment before Christ, yet did not accept or faithfully live the fullness of the gospel of Jesus Christ as taught by the LDS Church. These people are described as those who lived "honorable lives"[44] or accepted Christ, but were not "valiant in the testimony of Jesus."[45] This may include non-LDS people who believe in Jesus, but refused to accept the LDS laws and ordinances, as well as LDS members who did not faithfully keep all of the covenants they made with God in baptism and/or the temple.

The third and last kingdom of glory, the telestial kingdom, is prepared for those who completely rejected Christ and His message in mortality and in the spirit world, but were still faithful in the premortal world by choosing Jesus's plan to come to earth.[46]

This is normally where the missionaries will stop, but Latter-day Saints also believe there is a fourth kingdom, but it is not a kingdom of glory. This kingdom is that of the devil, Lucifer, and all of his angels who were cast out from heaven for rebellion. Sorted into this kingdom are those who had a perfect knowledge and testimony of God, yet rejected Him with a full and complete knowledge and understanding. This is what is

---

42 Doctrine and Covenants 132:19-20.
43 Doctrine and Covenants 132:24.
44 *Preach My Gospel*, 53.
45 Doctrine and Covenants 76:79.
46 See Doctrine and Covenants 76:81-86.

known as "outer darkness." More details are given in Doctrine and Covenants 76:32-33.

At this point, the curtain falls. Those who are righteous will live in a kingdom of glory and happiness in heaven, depending on their faithfulness, and those who knowingly and willingly reject God will spend eternity in outer darkness. From there, the Latter-day Saints speculate that those who receive the highest kingdom of glory, i.e., exaltation in the celestial kingdom, will be able to have spiritual offspring in the eternities, or a "continuation of the seeds forever and ever."[47] They will continue the lineage of God's family into eternity. Just as these faithful Latter-day Saints were spirit children of Heavenly Father and Heavenly Mother, sealed husbands and wives hope to have spirit children.

There is disagreement as to the particulars of being exalted, whether they will create their own planets, galaxies, and universes, or whether they will simply continue to submit to God the Father and create spirit children for His creation. Regardless, LDS members see God's Plan of Salvation as a continuous cycle that repeats over the eons as new spirit children are born who will reach exaltation and eternal life, and who in turn create their children who work toward the goal of reaching eternal life and exaltation, in "one eternal round."[48]

Having laid out the entire LDS Plan of Salvation, I will now provide a response from a biblical perspective.

A Biblical Response

Now that we have seen the Latter-day Saint understanding of God's plan for us, let us see how it differs from a historic understanding of what the Bible teaches. The Bible differs in many respects from the LDS doctrine of the premortal world,

---

47   Doctrine and Covenants 132:19
48   See 1 Nephi 10:19; Alma 7:19-20 (Book of Mormon).

and the consequences of this doctrine are like ripples in a pond that grow and spread to affect everything around them.

The first line in the book of Genesis says, *In the beginning God created the heavens and the earth* (Genesis 1:1). This indicates several important doctrines:

1. Everything came into being as it is during the creation.

2. The creation was when time began (or there wasn't anything happening in a sequence of time before the beginning).

3. At the beginning, God created humankind.

The last point is confirmed by Zechariah, who declares, *Thus says the Lord, who stretches out the heavens, lays the foundation of the earth, and forms the spirit of man within him:"* (Zechariah 12:1).

The Bible passage most commonly used by the Latter-day Saints to support their claim that we lived with God in heaven during our premortal existence is Jeremiah 1:5: *Before I formed you in the womb I knew you.* But is that what this verse is saying? When we consider the fact that God is eternal and is not bound by the limits of time as we mortals are, we understand that God sees and knows all things that happen, whether past, present, or future. God did not need to see Jeremiah in front of Him to know him before his birth. God, who is the timeless and eternal One, does not experience time as we do. He chose Jeremiah before he was born and saw him in his role as a prophet long before his parents or his parents' parents stepped foot on the earth.

Regarding the LDS belief that every human is a literal spirit child of Heavenly Father and Heavenly Mother, the Bible teaches that we are not literal children of God by nature. It is only possible that those who believe in Christ may become children by adoption, by grace alone through faith alone in Christ alone. These are those who *received Him,* and to them God *gave the right to become children of God* (John 1:12). Regarding the moment we came into existence, the Bible teaches that God formed us within our mother's womb. The psalmist gives praise to the Lord because of this: *For You formed my inward parts; You covered me in my mother's womb* (Psalm 139:13) and *Your hands have made me and fashioned me* (Psalm 119:73).

The Bible confirms this when describing how Adam came alive for the first time at creation: *And the LORD God formed man of the dust of the ground, and breathed into his nostrils the breath of life; and man became a living being* (Genesis 2:7). Consequently, Adam could not have previously been the archangel Michael, and nowhere does Scripture teach this.

The teaching that the fall of Adam and Eve was set up as a contradictory situation where they either could abstain from the fruit of the tree of the knowledge of good and evil, or they could partake of the fruit and have children, but could not do both simultaneously, is also absent from the Genesis account. It is entirely possible, at least hypothetically, that Adam and Eve could have remained faithful and could have had offspring in the garden of Eden. It is only the Book of Mormon that forces this contradiction.

The fall of Adam and Eve is considered by most of Christianity to be a true fall that brought pain, death, sickness, suffering, ruin, and sin upon all mankind. Paul wrote to his fellow believers in Ephesus and remarked about their spiritual state prior to being saved as being *dead in trespasses and sins, fulfilling the desires of the flesh*, and being *children of wrath* (Ephesians 2:1-3). In summary, we were spiritually lost.

Thankfully, for true Christians, those who trust in Christ and have been born again, this was only possible because *God, who is rich in mercy, because of His great love with which He loved us, even when we were dead in trespasses, made us alive together with Christ (by grace you have been saved), and raised us up together, and made us sit together in the heavenly places in Christ Jesus* (Ephesians 2:4-6). We were saved from the state of open rebellion against God and were made into new creations (2 Corinthians

5:17). Born again believers are no longer under God's wrath, but are abounding in His grace and redeeming love (1 Timothy 1:12-17).

On the topic of the atonement of Christ, there are two significant departures from the Bible in LDS beliefs. The first is that they believe that Jesus bled from every pore of His body in the garden of Gethsemane. The second is that they believe that Jesus paid the price for our sins while praying in the garden of Gethsemane. Christians recognize that Jesus's suffering in the garden was indeed a reality, but they do not believe that this was when He paid the debt for our sins. Christ's suffering and death upon the cross is the event that reconciled man with God (see 1 Peter 2:24; 1 Corinthians 1:18; Colossians 1:20; Ephesians 2:16).

While Christ's prayer in the garden of Gethsemane resulted in agony to the point where *His sweat became like great drops of blood falling down to the ground* (Luke 22:44), this did not mean He was bleeding from every pore. If that were the case, Jesus would have been absolutely drenched in blood, but the account does not explicitly say this, nor is it implied by how others interacted with Him after His prayer.

Regarding the various kingdoms of glory in heaven as believed by the Latter-day Saints, it is true that Jesus said in John 14 that He would go to prepare a place for His disciples. However, while the Bible does indicate that there will be rewards according to our works, it does not indicate that there are rigid divisions in heaven that separate the saints based on faithfulness. The only passage that LDS missionaries point to as evidence of the celestial, terrestrial, and telestial kingdoms is 1 Corinthians 15. The King James Version of the Bible speaks of the "glory of the celestial" and the "glory of the terrestrial" (1 Corinthians 15:40).

Upon first glance, it may certainly seem as if the Bible mentions the celestial and terrestrial kingdoms. However, when Joseph Smith was working on his "translation" of the Bible, he added a phrase to verse 40 so that it states the following (changes from the King James Version are in bold): "Also celestial bodies, and bodies terrestrial, **and bodies telestial**; but the glory of the celestial, one; and the terrestrial, another; **and the telestial, another**."[49] This may seem to make sense to LDS audiences since the following verse describes "one glory of the sun, and another glory of the moon, and another glory of the stars," yet only two bodies are mentioned in the previous verse (celestial bodies and bodies terrestrial), so there must have been a third body that was missing or removed. However, if we examine the Greek words translated into English as "celestial" and "terrestrial," they are the words *epourania* (based on *epouranios*, meaning roughly "of heaven" or "in the heavenly sphere") and *epigeia* (based on *epigeios*, meaning roughly "of the earth"), respectively. Most modern Bible translators, intending to more accurately translate from the original Greek for modern English readers, translate these words as "heavenly" and "earthly," respectively.

Thus, the passage is not speaking of different realms of glory, but it is comparing the difference in majesty between bodies one can find in the cosmos (*sun . . . moon . . .* and *the stars*, 1 Corinthians 15:41) and bodies on earth (*men . . . animals . . . fish . . . birds*, 1 Corinthians 15:39). Translating these words as "celestial" and "terrestrial" is not a bad or faulty translation whatsoever – if it is understood what the King James translators originally meant. However, these are words that are rarely used in common speech today and don't clearly express the meaning of Paul's writing. To help avoid such confusion and incorrect interpretations, Bible scholars recommend not to rely on a single translation of the Bible. Instead, we should rely on multiple translations (if one has that opportunity) and compare them to get the correct sense of a passage.[50]

---

49   1 Corinthians 15:40 (Joseph Smith Translation).

50   About this passage, see Robert M. Bowman Jr., "Three Kingdoms of Glory: Joseph Smith, 1 Corinthians 15, and Doctrine and Covenants 76," https://mit. irr.org/three-kingdoms-of-glory-joseph-smith-1-corinthians-15-and-doctrine-covenants-76.

Continuing to the Latter-day Saint's view of outer darkness, the Bible paints a different picture regarding hell. Whether we like it or not, hell is a place that is described in Scripture as a reality. It may or may not be literally covered in fire and brimstone or with demons in cloaks and scythes, and we aren't even sure where it is, or if it even has a specific spatial location, but it is a real state of being that is not just reserved for very few. In the New Testament, Jesus spoke of the reality of hell, whether in "Hades," roughly translated as the world of spirits or of the dead, or in "Gehenna," the everlasting abode of the condemned and that there are many who are going there.

In fact, Jesus spoke of hell more than any other figure or author in the New Testament. Jesus spoke of it most clearly in His parable of the rich man and Lazarus as relayed in Luke 16. In this parable, the rich man enjoyed the good things of this life, but did not know the Lord, while Lazarus was a poor man who did not enjoy such pleasures and suffered greatly with sores and hunger. The two died, and Jesus said that the rich man *died and was buried. And being in torments in Hades, he lifted up his eyes* (Luke 16:22-23). While this is a parable and there is debate as to whether this is referring to a real event or is merely a story for illustration, Jesus in no way seems to allegorize or trivialize the plight of the rich man, and it is not just given for effect.

Jesus here describes the possibility of being in *torments* after death as a vivid reality that is not simply for those who commit the most heinous sins imaginable, or even just for those who commit the unpardonable sin of denying the Holy Spirit. Hell (Hades or Gehenna) is described as the abode of those who seek after the things of this world and do not have any concern for the gospel of Christ or of heavenly things. While the LDS missionaries may say that this is speaking of Spirit Prison and not an eternal hell, there doesn't seem to be any hope for the rich man in this torment. He cries out to Abraham for mercy, but he finds no reprieve. There are also no missionaries there to teach him the gospel so he can pass from "Spirit Prison" to "Spirit Paradise." He is in a state that cannot be changed, altered, or relieved.

On this same subject of life after death, there is no indication that there will be a second chance to accept Christ in the afterlife. Scripture describes the gospel as being preached and accepted in mortality. There is no missionary work in the afterlife, and being baptized on behalf of our deceased ancestors does not bring them closer to God. Paul's description of being *baptized for the dead* in 1 Corinthians 15:29 is a passing mention and does not seem to indicate that Paul is commending, sanctioning, or commanding such a practice. It is a minor point in a longer discourse with the purpose of refuting those who deny the idea of resurrection. To base an entire system and set of doctrines around a single short, cryptic, and unclear statement is a very dangerous way to interpret God's Word. That is one reason why no notable Christian denomination (apart from fringe groups) has historically ever practiced baptism by proxy for the deceased.

As for how the Bible describes our state after death, we either die in Christ and are immediately brought into the presence of God, or we die rejecting Christ entirely and have a fate similar to that of the rich man in Luke 16. Scripture says that *it is appointed for men to die once, but after this the judgment* (Hebrews 9:27), and this is the case with us. All of humanity, without exception, will die and be judged before God. However, Christians have the blessed hope that once we die, if we have truly trusted in Christ alone to save us from our sins, we will be justified (declared righteous), just as *Abraham believed God, and it was accounted to him for righteousness* (Romans 4:3; see also Genesis 15:6).

Those who trust in Christ alone to save them will be judged righteous because the Father will see us clothed in the perfect righteousness of Jesus. Those who die without knowing or trusting Christ will not have this comfort, and they will be judged based on their own "righteousness" to determine whether they enter heaven or not. However, we know that *all have sinned and fall short of the glory of God* (Romans 3:23), and according to God's perfect standard of holiness, *There is none righteous, no, not one. . . . There is none who does good, no, not one* (Romans 3:10, 12). It is vital for all people everywhere to trust in Christ now while they still have the chance – because they will not be able to enter God's presence based upon what they do or by any other way. Only the blood of Christ can cleanse us and make us perfect when we stand before God to be judged.

I hope and pray that you will read God's Word closely and view it, as the psalmist does, as *a lamp to [your] feet and a light to [your] path* (Psalm 119:105). While the LDS missionaries may claim to have answers to questions that evangelicals do not, such as where we came from and where we are going, if we rest upon what the Word of God says, and if we *sanctify the Lord God in [our] hearts*, we will *always be ready to give a defense to everyone who asks [us] a reason for the hope that is in [us]* (1 Peter 3:15). As Christians, our hope is eternal life in Christ and the promise that we will rise with Him in glory at the last day because of His righteousness and faithfulness. When we have this hope, we realize that any substitute cannot even come close to approaching it.

May the Lord bless you in your Christian walk and in your interactions with our LDS friends – many who are desperately seeking this same hope.

* * * *

Matthew Eklund was born and raised in the LDS faith in northern Utah. After serving a two-year mission to the Belgium-Brussels/Netherlands Mission, he earned a BS in Mechanical Engineering and an MS in Nuclear Engineering at the University of Utah, and a PhD in Nuclear Engineering and Science at Rensselaer Polytechnic Institute. He is currently a researcher at Idaho National Laboratory in Idaho Falls, Idaho. He co-hosts the *Outer Brightness* podcast, where he shares his experiences of transitioning from the LDS faith to Protestant Christianity. He enjoys reading, gaming, and spending time with his wife. *Ghostbusters* is and has been his favorite film franchise since childhood.

Chapter 6

Missionary Lesson Three:
The Gospel of Jesus Christ

By Paul Nurnberg

M y upbringing in Salt Lake City, Utah, was idyllic. I would spend summer afternoons with friends climbing to caves in the foothills above the city, catching guppies, swimming, riding bikes, and playing sports. We would stay out until sunset, when hues of fierce orange and flamingo pink faded to dusky purples above the shadow-blackened Oquirrh Mountains, and the cool of night descended on our beautiful valley.

It wasn't all childhood innocence, though. My friends and I would scrounge quarters so we could play Super Mario Brothers at the Gas 'N Go or to gorge ourselves on broken fruit pies sold out of the back window of the bakery as "quality rejects" for forty cents a dozen. In my case, I would steal change from my mom's purse, from the family's "swear and fight jar," and, when I had exhausted those resources, from my dad's beloved coin collection that he had been keeping since he was a child.

That last one prompted an investigation. My older sister told on me. She had seen me swiping change from the family jar.

As retaliation, I gathered up some of my mom's red t-shirt paint and most of my sisters' Barbie and Ken dolls, and I headed to the front porch. Once there, I proceeded to pull the arms, legs, and heads off the dolls and add t-shirt paint to create a scene of plastic carnage, which put my sisters in tears, and my mom, too, as she didn't know how to deal with me. That day, I dreaded the return of my dad from work. My sisters jokingly refer to it now as "The Great Barbie Massacre of 1986," but I'm still appalled at the level of my depravity at age eight. Sid from *Toy Story* triggers me.

When I was nine, we moved to the suburbs. I quickly secured a reputation as a troublemaker in our close-knit, mostly Mormon neighborhood. I had learned from a friend what it means to "flash" someone, and to my friend's delight and laughter, I promptly flashed the girls next door. Mormons can be good, forgiving people. The parents of the neighbor girls still allowed me to be friends with their son and hang out at their house, despite their reservations about me. I returned their trust one afternoon by sneaking into their oldest daughter's bedroom and using a Sharpie to draw mustaches on all of her Kirk Cameron posters. I was a skunk!

As a teenager, I continued my rebelliousness, along with two other friends. I tried beer for the first time with one friend. It was a Coors Light that he had pilfered from his stepdad's mini-fridge and had kept hidden for a week in the shade behind their shed. One hot summer day, he jumped the fence between our back-yards and we took turns gagging through sips from the golden can. That warm beer is still the worst thing I have ever tasted.

The three of us ran amok. We made a deal with a bar owner that if we bought food (Philly cheesesteaks, fried mushrooms, and "near beers"), he would let us spend early summer afternoons before Happy Hour playing pool in his establishment. Our curse-word laden billiards afternoons lasted for several weeks until a cop saw us going in one afternoon, put a stop to it, and alerted our parents. We were once threatened with expulsion from school because we had disrupted a school band performance by launching paper airplanes from the top row of the auditorium. One of the airplanes floated down and came to rest right next to the conductor's podium.

Another time, we all got arrested for vandalism. One of us had poured a pot of soup onto a neighbor's car because their kid threw rocks at us while we played basketball. The others had been present and tried to help cover it up by creating the alibi that we couldn't have done it because we had all spent the night at my house. A police car in front of the house on a Sunday morning solidified my reputation.

After church that day, my parents and I had a tense meeting with the bishop. I had been ordained a deacon, and I was barred from passing or receiving the sacrament of the Lord's Supper for several months. All this was compounded by lies told to my parents, the bishop, school officials, and the police. When my exasperated mom asked me why I caused so much trouble, all I could manage to say was, "I don't know." Although I had not yet read Augustine's *Confessions*, the cold realization that I enjoyed rebellion rattled against the walls of my mind that day and added to my guilt. Why couldn't I just be a good kid?

Later on, I spent a couple years racked with guilt. I had walked to the very edge of the sexual-sin cliff. I had not careened over the edge, but I hadn't exactly backed away from the precipice either. I had been taught that sexual sin was only surpassed in severity by murder and denying the Holy Ghost.[51] That guilt set me on a course to learn what grace feels like. During a routine interview with the bishop (a different bishop than before), he

---

51   See Alma 39:5 (Book of Mormon).

asked me if there was any sin in my life that required confession. I knew that based on the teachings of the Church, what I had done required confession, but I lied.

As I walked home that day, the hot summer sun felt like the fires of hell licking at my neck – and Mormons don't even believe in hell! Convicted, I turned around, walked back to the church, and sheepishly knocked on the bishop's door. I confessed what I had done – all that I had done – in a torrent of admissions. I included all that I have already mentioned, as well as a stolen basketball, calling a kid fat during a church basketball game because he had made me mad, skipping religion class to go to breakfast with friends, and drinking coffee.

When I finished, he just looked at me with compassion, and then he read to me from the Book of Mormon about Alma the Younger's conversion.[52] He then said, "Paul, you seem like you've been very troubled over these things, and that is a part of repentance. Confessing to me is another. But I think that Heavenly Father has already forgiven you for what you've done. Now you need to learn to forgive yourself." When I left his office for the second time that day, I felt lighter than air.

Three years later, that same bishop would shepherd me through the process of submitting my application to serve as an LDS missionary. On the eve of my final missionary worthiness interview with my stake president, I went out to play pool with some friends and drank alcohol. I had broken the Word of Wisdom. The next morning as I confessed my latest sin, I tried to minimize it by saying that it was only a "small sip." My stake president delayed submitting my application for three months.

You may have noticed a pattern in my story: sin, guilt, confession – repeat. I continued that sin/repentance cycle throughout my mission, confessing to my mission president indiscretions that I had forgotten about, but which, in the context of a mission

---

52   See Alma 36 (Book of Mormon).

in which strict obedience is stressed, came rushing back to plague my mind with guilt. I also reconfessed sins that I had already covered with other authorities, exasperating my mission president. He also spoke to me about grace and forgiveness. As a missionary, I was taught and believed that people would only accept my preaching of the "restored gospel" if I was worthy. Not getting up by 6:30 a.m. or not being back in our apartment by 9:30 p.m., thinking about home too much, harboring feelings of anger at my companion, or any other infraction of the mission rules or sin of omission kept me bound in chains of guilt and feeling unworthy.

What to Expect When LDS Missionaries Teach Lesson Three

After my LDS mission to Hungary, I met my wife, Angela. She had recently converted to Mormonism. She was baptized into the LDS Church just two weeks before my return from the mission, which we saw as providential. We maintained a long-distance relationship for six months (before the days of free cellular long distance) and racked up massive phone bills. After Christmas in 1999, I moved to the greater Cincinnati area to be closer to her. The following year, we married in the Bountiful Utah Temple on a beautiful spring day.

We spent the first ten years of our married life as active Latter-day Saints. For many of those years, we were happy Mormons. She had two young daughters before we met. I adopted them, and we were all sealed as an eternal family in the same temple where we married. We added three more children to our family – a boy and two more girls.

During the early years of our marriage, my scrupulosity about my sins remained, and Angela struggled with teachings about the sin/repentance cycle. It became clear to her just how starkly different this LDS teaching was from the teachings of her Southern Baptist upbringing. About a year and a half after we married, I had what Latter-day Saints colloquially call a "faith crisis." Mormons encourage each other to put questions for which they don't have answers on a metaphorical bookshelf. We can occasionally pull them down to examine them and try to find answers, but we should not throw the baby out with the bathwater. We should stay in the boat – don't leave the Church.[53] A faith crisis is when that metaphorical bookshelf collapses.

Early in our marriage, Angela told me that the LDS missionaries had answered perennial questions she'd had. She specifically mentioned "once saved, always saved" as a doctrine that she had struggled to accept as a teenager. Even though we both had growing doubts about the LDS Church, we tried to be good Latter-day Saints. We taught children's Sunday school together, and we each held various other callings in our LDS congregation.

Communication about religion was really good in those first few years. With her Christian background, Angela taught me a lot. She didn't always see doctrinal questions through Mormon lenses, and we had many stimulating conversations. After my initial LDS faith crisis, I was determined to rebuild my faith on the rock of Jesus Christ. As I did so, the writing on the wall became clear: if I had Jesus, I didn't need the LDS Church. However, that was not something I could entertain. I tried desperately to make myself believe that Joseph Smith really was God's prophet. I spent far too many hours focused on him instead of on Jesus.

Smith was an idol to me in those years. That led to guilt. As the husband, I was supposed to lead my family in matters of faith, but I was reading books that told the true history of Joseph Smith – and my belief in him as a prophet was gone. I began to hide what I really thought from Angela and our children. It would be a major sin if I led them away from the truth.

---

53   Russell M. Ballard, "Stay in the Boat and Hold On!" *Ensign*, November 2014, 89-92.

Our different backgrounds became a wedge between us, whereas they had previously been a strength. I could see her longing for blessed assurance. She had a deep need for the rest that was available only in Jesus. Unanswered questions compounded. What would become of us? We had been married for eternity in the temple! If one or both of us left the LDS Church, what would that mean for our relationship? Communication broke down. Reticence replaced openness. Defensiveness, fear, and shame ruled.

In May of 2010, after a few years of strain in our relationship, Angela asked if we could have a straightforward, private conversation away from our children. We had both been feeling that we weren't growing in Christ, but I had been paralyzed by fear. I had been protective of my own LDS background – even though I didn't believe all that I said in defending it. I had told Angela several times that I would always be Mormon, that they were my people!

As we silently drove to a park and nature preserve near our home and walked into its interior, God's beauty surrounding us was no solace. I thought Angela was going to ask for a divorce. Eternal marriage is such a binding part of Mormon life that when couples leave, divorce often follows. Despite my fear and my attempts to fake confidence, what I feared most was going to happen anyway. What she did end up asking resulted in both of us kicking down walls and returning to healthy communication.

Latter-day Saints and Christians often struggle to have meaningful gospel conversations. We speak past each other because, although we use many of the same words, our definitions of those words differ. This is especially true of the word "gospel." Mormons believe that the true gospel of Jesus Christ was lost from the earth for almost two millennia. In Lesson One of *Preach My Gospel*, LDS missionaries refer to this time of lost truth and authority as "The Great Apostasy."[54] They teach that the gospel had to be restored through the ministry of Joseph

---

54   *Preach My Gospel*, 35-36.

Smith. The content of this "restored gospel" is summarized as follows: The gospel of Jesus Christ is the only way to eternal life and exaltation. The first principles and ordinances of His gospel are faith in Jesus Christ, repentance, baptism by immersion for the remission of sins, and the gift of the Holy Ghost. We must then endure to the end.[55]

Faith, repentance, baptism, Holy Spirit, endure to the end – these are all Bible words; but do Latter-day Saints mean the same thing Christians mean when they use them? It's important to unpack what the LDS missionaries mean when they use these terms, and to listen closely to how they define them.

Faith: Let's Talk about Faith Alone or Faith + Works

When Angela and I were newly married, I worked two jobs to support our family and save money for schooling. One evening, while delivering pizza, I was listening to *The Bible Answer Man* radio program hosted by Hank Hanegraaff. Imagine this as if you're watching a scene in a movie. It begins with the camera focusing on a small, white Ford Escort wagon from high above. The car crests a hill and turns onto a street lined with large, beautiful homes. As the car proceeds down the street and away from the camera, the camera zooms in until you can see clearly through the rear window, and suddenly you're in the car. The crackled hum of the AM radio fades into clarity.

Hank takes a call from a Latter-day Saint listener who asks a question to try to understand how Protestants can believe that they are saved by grace alone, through faith alone, in Christ alone – without any works. Hank answers that Christians don't believe that good works are necessary to be saved, but that they are evidence that a person is saved. The caller presses him to explain why James wrote, *Even so faith, if it hath not works, is*

---

55   *Preach My Gospel*, 67.

dead, being alone (James 2:17 KJV), if works are unnecessary for salvation. The discussion progresses to the doctrines of justification and sanctification. The camera angle is now such that you seem to be the driver, and you slap your hand on the steering wheel. As you listen to Hank, you're as frustrated as the caller is as you try to understand the nuance of his explanation. You yell at the car radio, "It's all just semantics!"

Why did I place you in that car with me? I did so because I want you to zoom in even further so you can understand why I was so frustrated and why I yelled at my car radio. I want to take you into the Latter-day Saint heart. Back then, I would have rejected the idea that I believed in a false gospel of works righteousness. However, it is a charge that Mormons cannot easily escape. It leads them to ask questions such as the following:

- If the work of the cross is finished, if Christ did all the work and there is nothing for us to work for, then why do we have to "work out" our salvation with fear and trembling?

- Do Evangelicals believe they will get to heaven without doing any good works?

- Can salvation without works be true? Can there truly be no requirements for salvation?

What is the heart condition that lies beneath these questions? Latter-day Saints are taught that in some sense their own works will allow them to be judged worthy by God. They might even reject the way I phrased that, but if they haven't done the works, they don't expect salvation. Where do Mormons get the idea that their works help them put a finger on the scales of justice so that the righteous side outweighs the unrighteous side? They get it from their own scriptures and from the way that "faith" is defined for them.

In 1834, when the LDS Church was less than five years old, Joseph Smith and Sidney Rigdon began instructing elders in the fledgling church with a series of lessons that were later called the *Lectures on Faith*. In the following year, these lectures began to be published along with a collection of Joseph Smith's revelations. The resulting work was called the Doctrine and Covenants, which was accepted by the membership of the church as scripture during the October 1880 general conference. Until 1921, the *Lectures on Faith* made up the "Doctrine" portion of the Doctrine and Covenants. Although they were removed at that time, the *Lectures on Faith* retain an important place in LDS doctrinal understanding, especially as it relates to the *law of faith*.

The third Article of Faith of the LDS Church states: "We believe that through the Atonement of Christ, all mankind may be saved, by obedience to the laws and ordinances of the Gospel."[56] Faith is the first law of the "restored gospel." When I graduated from LDS seminary, a religion class taken by Mormon high schoolers, my stake president gave each of the graduates a hardcover copy of the *Lectures on Faith* with our names embossed on the front cover. I studied from that book extensively while I was on my mission.

> Faith is the topic of the first lecture, which states in regard to the law of faith:
>
> In a word, is there anything that you would have done, either physical or mental, if you had not previously believed? Are not all your exertions of every kind, dependent on your faith? Or may we not ask, what have you, or what do you possess, which you have not obtained by reason of your faith? Reflect and ask yourselves if these things are not so. Turn your thoughts on your own minds

---

56 Articles of Faith 3 (Pearl of Great Price).

and see if faith is not the moving cause of all action in yourselves; and if the moving cause in you, is it not in all other intelligent beings?[57]

The law of faith is echoed in *PMG*. LDS missionaries teach:

> Faith in Christ leads to action. It leads to sincere and lasting change. Having faith causes us *to try as hard as we can* to learn about and become more like our Savior with "unshaken faith in him, relying wholly upon the merits of him who is mighty to save" (2 Nephi 31:19). We want to learn His will and keep His commandments. Even though we will still make mistakes, we show our love for Him by striving through the power of Christ's Atonement to keep His commandments and *avoid sin*. We believe in Christ, and we believe that He wants us *to keep all His commandments. We show our faith by obeying Him.*[58] [italics added]

What's wrong with this? Didn't Jesus teach that one cannot serve two masters (Luke 16:13), and didn't the apostle Paul say that he was a bondservant of Christ and therefore indebted to Christ (Romans 1:1)? Christians do indeed believe that Jesus is Lord and that we should obey Him, so what's the difference? What is the heart issue that led me to cry out in frustration at my car radio?

The answer lies in how Mormons read Philippians 2:12: *Therefore, my beloved, as you have always obeyed, not as in my presence only, but now much more in my absence, work out your*

---

57   *Lectures on Faith.* (Salt Lake City: Deseret Book, 1985), 2-3. For more on the history of the *Lectures on Faith* see https://www.churchofjesuschrist.org/study/history/topics/lectures-on-faith?lang=eng.

58   *Preach My Gospel*, 62-63.

own salvation with fear and trembling. Are Christians supposed to live their lives in *fear and trembling* because they might not be found good enough to live in God's presence, or does the *fear and trembling* that Paul refers to come from the fact that it is the very God of heaven and earth *who works in you both to will and to do for His good pleasure* (Philippians 2:13)?[59] In the LDS system, one must have faith, which is not mere belief or even trust. For Latter-day Saints, faith is strictly a verb. It includes completing extrabiblical works that are requisites to receiving blessings.

Repentance: Let's Talk about Staircases and Ladders

In Christian circles, when someone gives their testimony of being born again, the person sometimes says that he was caught in a cycle of sin and would try to remove that sin from his life – often bargaining with God in prayer because the sin had gotten him into trouble: "Lord, if You get me out of this awful predicament, I'll do something for You." Often, the promises are forgotten and the sin continues. We also often hear these people proclaim that when they were born again, their hearts were truly changed and they realized the futility of bargaining with God.

LDS scriptures teach that "there is a law, irrevocably decreed in heaven before the foundations of this world, upon which all blessings are predicated – and when we obtain any blessing from God, it is by obedience to that law, upon which it is predicated."[60] In recent years, the messaging from some LDS leaders, and especially from LDS scholars at church-owned universities, has emphasized grace more. As a result, Mormons might contend that eternal life is a gift that no one can earn. One passage of LDS scripture that I memorized as a teenager

---

59   It is critical not to take Philippians 2:12 out of context and sever it from verse 13.
60   Doctrine and Covenants 130:20-21.

even states explicitly that eternal life is a gift; however, that same passage indicates that the gift is conditioned and predicated on an if/then statement: "If you keep my commandments and endure to the end you shall have eternal life, which gift is the greatest of all the gifts of God."[61] That if/then statement is the cause of the Mormon heart problem!

I have a sister who is still a Latter-day Saint. In 2020, she sent me a link to an episode from *Come Follow Me Insights*, a Book of Mormon Central podcast and YouTube channel. She included the following note with the link:

> Remember when we were talking about faith versus works and grace? I remember that you felt that in the LDS Church, we don't truly believe in being saved by grace. I was confused because if you listen to this podcast, this is what I remember being taught in seminary. We might still agree to disagree about what the LDS Church actually teaches.

On our podcast, *Outer Brightness*, Matthew Eklund, Michael Flournoy, and I responded to the *Come Follow Me Insights* episode.[62] In the episode to which my sister provided me the link, Brigham Young University professors Taylor Halverson and Tyler Griffin discuss 3 Nephi 12-16 from the Book of Mormon. In those chapters, the resurrected Jesus is said to have visited a people group in the Americas whom the Book of Mormon identifies as Nephites, and He supposedly delivers to them a modified version of the Sermon on the Mount. Professor Griffin suggests that the Beatitudes represent a staircase that leads the

---

61 Doctrine and Covenants 14:7.

62 Matthew Eklund, Michael Flournoy, and Paul Nurnberg, "Becoming Perfect: A Response to Book of Mormon Central's Come Follow Me Insights," January 3, 2021, in *Outer Brightness*, podcast audio, https://www.outerbrightnesspodcast.com/e/becoming-perfect-a-response-to-book-of-mormon-centrals-come-follow-me-insights/.

faithful step-by-step to perfection. Speaking about the whole staircase that is drawn out on the whiteboard behind him, he makes this statement: "This isn't a one-time event. This is actually a very long, repeating process. You do it again and again and again."[63] As he makes this statement, the video shows an unending spiral staircase as viewed from above and going even higher, giving the appearance of a continual, cyclical climb.

Christians wrestle with the sin nature throughout their lives, and they feel remorse when they sin. So what's the difference? Why did I feel hopeless as a Latter-day Saint? Mormons are taught that they must repent daily and abandon their sins or their former sins will be held against them. LDS scripture explicitly teaches this:

> And the anger of God kindleth against the inhabitants of the earth; and none doeth good, for all have gone out of the way. And now, verily I say unto you, I, the Lord, will not lay any sin to your charge; go your ways and sin no more; but unto that soul who sinneth shall the former sins return, saith the Lord your God.[64]

The goal of every believer in the "restored gospel" is to become like God – to become gods themselves, as Joseph Smith taught.[65] When people read the Bible with the eyes of a child, their consciences are pricked and they recognize that God is, and always

---

63   Tyler Griffin and Taylor Halverson, "Come Follow Me (Insights into 3 Nephi 12-16, September 21–27)," *Book of Mormon Central*, September 14, 2020, video, https://www.youtube.com/watch?app=desktop&t=2087&v=gBoa EQh_dTA&feature=youtu.be.

64   Doctrine and Covenants 82:6-7.

65   Joseph Fielding Smith, ed., *Teachings of the Prophet Joseph Smith* (Salt Lake City: Deseret Book, 1969), 348. "You have got to learn how to be gods yourselves, and to be kings and priests to God, the same as all gods have done before you, namely, by going from one small degree to another, and from a small capacity to a great one; from grace to grace, from exaltation to exaltation, until you attain to the resurrection of the dead, and are able to dwell in everlasting burnings, and to sit in glory, as do those who sit enthroned in everlasting power."

will be, greater than we could ever hope to be; God is perfect. Even Joseph Smith understood the difficulty of the task he was placing before his followers. In the very same sermon in which he told them that they have to learn to become gods, he told them this:

> When you climb up a ladder, you must begin at the bottom, and ascend step by step, until you arrive at the top; and so it is with the principles of the Gospel – you must begin with the first and go on until you learn all the principles of exaltation. But *it will be a great while after you have passed through the veil before you will have learned them*. It is not all to be comprehended in this world; *it will be a great work to learn our salvation and exaltation even beyond the grave.*[66] [italics added]

Latter-day Saints who understand the impossibility of the goal set before them know that they cannot have blessed assurance – neither in this life nor in the life to come. It is a long and repeating process, a never-ending climb up a staircase or a ladder. Mormons often caricature the Christian view of heaven. They suggest that Christians believe they will just float around on clouds and play harps for eternity, or that they view God as narcissistic for doing all things for His own glory – including accepting praise for eternity.

Please consider the state of a person's heart who says things like that. What must they believe about God? How must they feel about God? What must they think about their own works and worthiness? I'm trying to bring you into the Latter-day Saint heart so that you will love them and reach them with the true gospel.

---

66   Joseph Fielding Smith, ed., *Teachings*, 348.

Baptism: Let's Talk about Promises

Latter-day Saints are taught that baptism is the gate by which they must enter. The Book of Mormon states:

> For the gate by which ye should enter is repentance and baptism by water; and then cometh a remission of your sins by fire and by the Holy Ghost. And then are ye in this strait and narrow path which leads to eternal life; yea, ye have entered in by the gate; ye have done according to the commandments of the Father and the Son; and ye have received the Holy Ghost, which witnesses of the Father and the Son, unto the fulfilling of the promise which he hath made, that if ye entered in by the way ye should receive.[67]

Are you picking up on the pattern? Woven throughout LDS scripture and teaching is the picture of a very long path, ladder, or stairway one must climb to achieve the goal of ultimate salvation and glorification, which they call exaltation.

So far, we have covered the first *laws* of the "restored gospel" that Mormons must obey: faith and repentance. While Mormons are taught that faith is an action word and that repentance also requires them to act, these are largely internal aspects of a person's life. The first *ordinances* of the "restored gospel" – baptism and confirmation – are external acts.

When they receive an ordinance such as baptism, Latter-day Saints are taught that they enter into a covenant with God. Covenants are defined as two-way promises. The person receiving baptism promises to do certain things, and in return for the person faithfully keeping that *covenant*, God promises to provide certain blessings. The "restored gospel" is one of reciprocity: do *this* and you shall receive *that*.

---

67   2 Nephi 31:17b-18 (Book of Mormon).

When I was baptized in 1986 at the age of eight, I was taught that my past transgressions had been washed away. Now it was my duty to repent of all my future sins in order to remain "worthy," and it was also my duty to renew my baptismal covenant each week by partaking of the sacrament of the Lord's Supper.

What are the promises that Latter-day Saints make at baptism and renew each Sunday? The content of the baptismal covenant for Latter-day Saints is found in two passages in the Book of Mormon. At baptism, they promise to take the name of Christ upon them and to be obedient for the remainder of their lives. The first passage that defines the baptismal covenant for them states:

> And under this head ye are made free, and there is no other head whereby ye can be made free. There is no other name given whereby salvation cometh; therefore, I would that ye should take upon you the name of Christ, all you that have entered into the covenant with God that ye should be obedient unto the end of your lives. And it shall come to pass that whosoever doeth this shall be found at the right hand of God, for he shall know the name by which he is called; for he shall be called by the name of Christ. And now it shall come to pass, that whosoever shall not take upon him the name of Christ must be called by some other name; therefore, he findeth himself on the left hand of God.[68]

The next passage from the Book of Mormon that delineates the promises of the baptismal covenant states:

> And it came to pass that he said unto them: Behold, here are the waters of Mormon (for thus

---

68   Mosiah 5:8-10 (Book of Mormon).

were they called) and now, as ye are desirous to
come into the fold of God, and to be called his
people, and are willing to bear one another's burdens, that they may be light; yea, and are willing
to mourn with those that mourn; yea, and comfort
those that stand in need of comfort, and to stand as
witnesses of God at all times and in all things, and
in all places that ye may be in, even until death,
that ye may be redeemed of God, and be numbered
with those of the first resurrection, that ye may
have eternal life – Now I say unto you, if this be the
desire of your hearts, what have you against being
baptized in the name of the Lord, as a witness
before him that ye have entered into a covenant
with him, that ye will serve him and keep his commandments, that he may pour out his Spirit more
abundantly upon you?[69]

Aren't the baptismal covenants that Latter-day Saints take upon
themselves laudable goals? Who doesn't want friends and family
to gather around them in times of trouble and provide help, peace,
and comfort? Isn't that what Jesus meant when He commanded
His followers to love one another as He had loved them (John
13:34), or to love their neighbors as themselves (Mark 12:31)?

If you're reading this book, you probably have Mormon friends
and acquaintances. You likely know them to be kind and generous
people, but what motivates them to kindness and generosity? Is it
primarily to give glory to God for the abundance of His match-
less grace, or is it primarily to merit glory (achieve exaltation)
for themselves? It might be a mixture of both in their minds, but
they are keeping a promise they have made – a promise upon
which their own salvation and exaltation depends.

---

69   Mosiah 18:8-10 (Book of Mormon).

The LDS teaching about covenants is covered more fully in a later chapter, but it is important to introduce the concept when discussing baptism. The LDS missionaries teach:

> Covenants place us under a strong obligation to honor our promises to God. We should desire to worthily receive the covenants that God offers us and then strive to keep them. Our covenants remind us to repent every day of our lives, relying upon Jesus Christ. By loving the Lord, keeping His commandments, and loving and serving others we receive and retain a remission of our sins.[70]

Did you catch the double bind? They must be worthy and be judged worthy by their bishop and other leaders to receive ordinances. Once they receive the ordinances, they must remain worthy by keeping their covenants. What happens if they receive an ordinance unworthily? Is it valid? Can they make it valid by future obedience? Can they be worthy in the future by keeping covenants if they weren't worthy to receive one of the ordinances in the first place?

Consider the teaching that covenants place them "under a strong obligation" to keep their part of the covenant in light of Doctrine and Covenants 82:7, which I quoted earlier. Latter-day Saints are often asked to serve other members of their congregations in various ways. Maybe a Mormon mother is asked to take a meal to the home of a family who just experienced the death of a loved one, or where a family member is ill. Maybe a Mormon father is asked to spend a Saturday away from his family helping another family load or unload a moving truck. Suppose that the Mormon mother who was asked to provide the meal faces the challenge of feeding her own family on their

---

70   *Preach My Gospel*, 63.

budget, let alone another family. Suppose that the Mormon father is a coach for his daughter's soccer team and must choose between coaching his daughter's team one Saturday morning or helping someone move.

How many of us love our neighbors, let alone our enemies, perfectly? The motivation behind our actions matters. What happens in a person's heart and mind when they are trying as hard as they can to keep their covenants, and they see others who, from their perspective, don't seem to be trying nearly as hard? It can lead to legalism and judgment. Many former Mormons will tell you that was a part of their experience. Again, I'm trying to bring you into the heart of the Latter-day Saint. Beneath their efforts to keep their baptismal covenant lies a deep despair and longing for peace and rest with God – for blessed assurance.

If a Latter-day Saint fails to keep their baptismal covenant, that is considered a sin of omission – something they should have done, but did not do. For that sin of omission, they must repent and not just try to be better, but they must seek to be perfect, or they will have other sins of commission for which they will need to repent. If they continue sinning, their scriptures teach them that the guilt of their former sins will return to them.

The challenge that Latter-day Saints face to always do the right thing is taught to them early, when they receive their first "CTR" ring. That acronym stands for "Choose the Right." It is reinforced in two hymns on this theme that are often sung in LDS services.[71]

Baptism removes the guilt of past transgressions. It places Latter-day Saints on the path of discipleship – the covenant path. While on that path, they must try to keep their promise to love and care for others in order to receive forgiveness for future sins and the constant companionship of the Holy Spirit.

---

71   "Do What Is Right" and "Choose the Right," *Hymns of the Church of Jesus Christ of Latter-day Saints* (Salt Lake City: Deseret Book Company, 1985), 237-238.

Baptism of Fire: Let's Talk about Companionship

Latter-day Saints are not taught that they are left alone to try to obey all the commandments and all their covenants in their own power. The second outward ordinance they receive is the gift of the Holy Spirit. The fifth LDS Article of Faith states, "We believe that a man must be called of God, by prophecy, and by the laying on of hands by those who are in authority, to preach the Gospel and administer in the ordinances thereof."[72] In *PMG*, "Lesson 1: The Restoration," LDS missionaries teach that God only considers those ordinances valid that are performed by LDS Church authorities.[73]

How does this ordinance benefit a person according to LDS teachings? Listen to what the missionaries will teach:

> The Holy Ghost has a sanctifying, cleansing effect upon us. Through the gift and power of the Holy Ghost, we can receive and retain a remission of sins through continued faith in Christ, repentance, and following the will of God and obedience to His commandments. Those who receive the gift of the Holy Ghost and remain worthy can enjoy His companionship throughout their lives.[74]

The companionship of the Holy Spirit is what gives us power to overcome sin and become sanctified. Notice, though, the two instances of the word "can" in the above paragraph. They are taught that while they have the right to the companionship of the Holy Spirit, it is not a guarantee; it is conditional upon a person's obedience to the LDS teachings. LDS scripture teaches, "I, the Lord, am bound when ye do what I say; but when ye do not what I say, ye have no promise."[75]

---

72 Articles of Faith 5 (Pearl of Great Price).

73 *Preach My Gospel*, 36.

74 *Preach My Gospel*, 65.

75 Doctrine and Covenants 82:10. Contrast this teaching with Romans 4:1-5.

This type of conditional teaching led Laura, a dear Christian sister and friend of mine, to declare that whatever promises LDS theology extends to Mormons with one hand, it takes away with the other. Laura witnesses to Mormons with us in online discussion groups, and she has spent countless hours reading popular LDS books to be sure she understands what they are taught – and her heart breaks for them.

In a 1996 General Conference address, LDS Apostle Dallin H. Oaks clearly stated the conditional nature of this ordinance. He said:

> The blessings available through the gift of the Holy Ghost are conditioned upon worthiness. "The Spirit of the Lord doth not dwell in unholy temples." Even though we have a right to his constant companionship, the Spirit of the Lord will dwell only with us when we keep the commandments. He will withdraw when we offend him by profanity, uncleanliness, disobedience, rebellion, or other serious sins.[76]

This concept of worthiness within LDS teachings is what leads many to feel dread, despair, and hopelessness when they think about the ultimate goal of the LDS system, which is to be found worthy to live in God's presence and to become gods.[77] Some will say – more so recently – that they do not feel such nihilism regarding the future state of their souls. They point out that 2 Nephi 31:19 states that they are supposed to rely "wholly on the merits of him who is mighty to save," so they say that their faith in Jesus will ensure their exaltation. Others will critique

---

76   Dallin H. Oaks, "Always Have His Spirit," *Ensign*, November 1996, 61.
77   "Becoming Like God," Gospel Topics Essays, The Church of Jesus Christ of Latter-day Saints, accessed November 17, 2022, https://www.churchofjesus-christ.org/study/manual/gospel-topics-essays/becoming-like-god?lang=eng.

Christians for believing that anyone could know for certain that they are one of the elect and are saved. What is the reason for these two seemingly opposed positions of assurance and lack of it in Latter-day Saint hearts and minds? The answer to that question lies in the final and lengthiest section of the staircase, ladder, or covenant path.

Endure to the End: Let's Talk about Assurance

In *PMG*, "Lesson 2: The Plan of Salvation," the LDS missionaries teach that heaven has three degrees of glory – the celestial, terrestrial, and telestial kingdoms – into which every person who has lived, or will ever live, on earth will be saved – to some degree.[78] In that sense, Latter-day Saints are Universalists. However, the segregation of souls into these three degrees of glory is done based on the works of people in this mortal life.[79] LDS missionaries also teach about who can enter the highest kingdom:

> The celestial kingdom has three heavens or degrees (see Doctrine and Covenants 131:1), and only those who have an eternal marriage, sealed by the Holy Spirit, can enter into the highest, which is exaltation (see Doctrine and Covenants 131:2). They will live in God's presence, become like Him, and receive a fullness of joy.[80]

This introduces further covenants that Latter-day Saints enter into within their temples. The *laws* and *ordinances* of the gospel that we have discussed up to this point are all preparatory and are performed outside of LDS temples. Once a person has received the ordinances of baptism, confirmation, and conferral

---

78 *Preach My Gospel*, 53.

79 Doctrine and Covenants 76:71-113.

80 *Preach My Gospel*, 53.

of the gift of the Holy Ghost, and remain worthy through church attendance and keeping their baptismal covenant, they may receive approval from their bishop and stake president to go to an LDS temple to receive further ordinances and enter into additional covenants.

These additional ordinances consist of a washing and anointing ritual, the endowment ceremony, and for couples, having their marriage sealed for time and eternity. Many Mormons believe that once they have been sealed to their spouse, they have received all the ordinances necessary to be exalted in the highest degree of the celestial kingdom and live in the presence of God for all eternity. But notice what is said about exaltation in the quoted paragraph from the missionary lesson above. An eternal marriage must be sealed by the Holy Spirit. That language foreshadows a further ordinance – the second anointing – about which many Mormons, especially until very recently, have been ignorant.

Why don't they know about this second anointing? The reason is that LDS Church leadership seeks to keep it secret, only obscurely referring to it as something that happens passively. This is how *PMG* defines the "Holy Spirit of Promise," which is a synonym for the second anointing ritual:

> The Holy Ghost is also referred to as the Holy Spirit
> of Promise (see Doctrine and Covenants 88:3).
> To be sealed by the Holy Spirit of Promise means
> that the Holy Ghost confirms that righteous acts,
> ordinances, and covenants are acceptable to God.
> The Holy Spirit of Promise testifies to the Father
> that the saving ordinances have been performed
> properly and that the covenants associated with
> them have been kept. Those who are sealed by
> the Holy Spirit of Promise receive all that the

Father has (see Doctrine and Covenants 76:51–60; Ephesians 1:13–14). *All covenants and performances must be sealed by the Holy Spirit of Promise if they are to be valid after this life* (see Doctrine and Covenants 132:7, 18–19, 26). Breaking covenants may remove the sealing (italics added).[81]

Notice that the above paragraph clearly teaches that unless covenants and performances are sealed by the Holy Spirit of Promise, they will not be valid in the next life. How does one have their ordinances and covenants sealed in that way? Is it a passive experience in which the Holy Spirit confirms to a person that they have been faithful enough to have their calling and election made sure? No. It is a by-invitation-only ordinance performed in a temple – the second anointing – and those who have received it are instructed never to speak about it to others.

An exact-phrase search of the LDS Church's website for "second anointing" results in only one hit. The teaching manual titled *Doctrines of the Gospel*, which is used to instruct college-aged students taking LDS Institutes of Religion courses, contains the following instruction for the teacher, confirming that the crowning ordinance in the LDS system is meant to be kept secret (emphasis in original):

Caution: Exercise caution while discussing the doctrine of having our calling and election made sure. Avoid speculation. Use only the sources given here and in the student manual. Do *not* attempt in any way to discuss or answer questions about the second anointing.[82]

---

81 *Preach My Gospel*, 97.
82 "Chapter 19: Eternal Life," *Doctrines of the Gospel: Teacher Manual,* (Salt Lake City: The Church of Jesus Christ of Latter-day Saints, 2000), 67, https://www.churchofjesuschrist.org/study/manual/doctrines-of-the-gospel/chapter-19?lang=eng.

While I was growing up, my parents held Family Home Evening – a program in the LDS Church in which parents set aside one evening a week to study and teach the "restored gospel" to their children. My parents taught us the LDS system of how to be saved and eventually exalted. I remember one time when my mom talked to us about eternal marriage. She said that because she and my dad had been sealed in the Salt Lake Temple, they had done all that was required to achieve exaltation. My dad reminded her that their marriage had not yet been "sealed by the Holy Spirit of Promise" and that they would have to endure to the end to have hope of eventually living in God's presence.

Scripture also addresses our need to endure to the end, but it has nothing to do with marriages and remaining married for eternity. *For we have become partakers of Christ if we hold the beginning of our confidence steadfast to the end* (Hebrews 3:14).

Since references to the second anointing ritual in LDS scripture and teaching are esoteric, many Latter-day Saints are left hungry. They are waiting for a passive experience of the Holy Spirit of Promise to confirm the validity of their ordinances and faithfulness in keeping their covenants, unaware that in all their striving, they will only be rewarded with assurance if they are invited to receive the second anointing. They either falsely believe they can have trust and assurance because they have done all they have been taught is necessary and are enduring, or they are left feeling that they are never doing enough, and they criticize anyone who thinks they can have blessed assurance.

How Should Christians Respond to the Lesson on the "Restored Gospel"?

In August of 2011, I was baptized in our Christian church at the age of thirty-three. Later that year, I attended Cincinnati Bible Seminary, studying for a Master of Divinity degree in

Biblical Studies. As God drew me to His Son alone for salvation, and as the Holy Spirit illuminated God's Word to help me understand that my works do not save me and that I am saved freely by Christ's death and resurrection, a question sat heavy on my heart: What would I say if I were face to face with my young LDS missionary self?

I wasn't speculating about using time travel to thwart God's providence and change the course of my life. I wondered what I would say to LDS missionaries who would knock on my door. I decided I would preach the true gospel of grace to them because knowing Jesus as my personal Savior changed my life. That determination and the stark contrast between the biblical good news and the "restored gospel" was brought home to me one night in the library at Cincinnati Christian University. I was reading Chuck Swindoll's book *The Grace Awakening* in which Swindoll quoted from D. Martyn Lloyd-Jones's book on Romans 6:

> The true preaching of the gospel of salvation by grace alone always leads to the possibility of this charge being brought against it [*Shall we continue in sin that grace may abound?* – Romans 6:1]. There is no better test as to whether a man is really preaching the New Testament gospel of salvation than this, that some people might misunderstand it and misinterpret it to mean that it really amounts to this, that because you are saved by grace alone it does not matter at all what you do; you can go on sinning as much as you like because it will redound all the more to the glory of grace. That is a very good test of gospel preaching. If my preaching and presentation of the gospel of salvation does not expose it to that misunderstanding, then it is not the gospel.[83]

---

83 Charles R. Swindoll, *The Grace Awakening* (Nashville: Thomas Nelson, 2003), 33-34.

There are many approaches that one can take in witnessing to Mormons. Indeed, there are many aspects of LDS doctrine and history that one can focus on in trying to remove the scales from their eyes and the shackles from their minds. In sharing my story and past beliefs, I have tried to bring you into the heart of Latter-day Saints. What they need more than anything else is the same thing all people need – the true gospel of Jesus Christ and Him crucified.

What to Do and Not to Do

This next section contains several dos and don'ts that are especially important for Christians as they prepare to meet with LDS missionaries in regard to *PMG*, "Lesson 3: The Gospel of Jesus Christ."

Do	Don't
Approach the LDS missionaries in love and kindness.	Allow a spirit of contention and superiority to taint your witness.
Take the time to get to know them individually and remember things they tell you about themselves and their families.	Think of the LDS missionaries and all Mormons as monolithic in their beliefs, thoughts, or needs.
Pray sincerely for them and for God to work in and through you as you prepare to meet with them.	Do not pray for them in the spirit of the "Zoramites," especially if you are praying with them present.[84]

---

84   See Alma 31:15-18 (Book of Mormon).

Do	Don't
Be a Berean.[85] Study to show yourself approved unto God.[86] Know the context and proper meaning of the Bible passages that LDS missionaries may use in teaching this lesson so that when they use them to try to suggest that they support their beliefs, you can lovingly challenge their understanding of the Bible passages:	"Bible bash" with them in anger, throwing passages back and forth to try to prove them wrong. They will likely not engage in that sort of exercise, and will view it as contention, which their scriptures teach them is of the devil.[87]

• John 3:16-17	• John 3:5
• Hebrews 11	• Romans 6:4
• James 2:17-26	• 1 Cor. 11:23-29
• Romans 3:23	
• 1 John 1:7-8	• Hebrews 5:4
• 2 Cor. 7:9-10	• John 3:1-8
• Matthew 3:13-17	• Galatians 5:22-23
• Acts 2:37-39	• John 14:26
• Luke 22:15-20	• Acts 19:1-6
	• Matthew 10:22

---

85   Acts 17:10-15.

86   2 Timothy 2:15.

87   3 Nephi 11:29 (Book of Mormon). Compare 2 Timothy 2:14 for the biblical injunction.

Do	Don't
Know the content of the true, biblical gospel of Jesus Christ, which is the preaching of the apostles of Christ and the message of the early church: • We are all sinners and fall short of the glory of God (Romans 3:23). • The penalty for sin is death, but God offers the free gift of eternal life through Jesus Christ (Romans 6:23). • Christ paid the penalty for our sins by His death on the cross (1 Corinthians 15:3). • He was placed in a tomb and resurrected on the third day (1 Corinthians 15:4). • Christ died for sinners, which shows God's love (Romans 5:8). • Those who are justified by faith have peace with God through Jesus Christ (Romans 5:1). • The righteousness believers have is not their own (Philippians 3:9). • Those who are in Christ are free from all condemnation (Romans 8:1).	Get bogged down in trying to teach them or convince them of the superiority of a particular theological system (Calvinism, Lutheranism, Arminianism, etc.).

* * * *

Paul Nurnberg was born and raised in the Salt Lake Valley in Utah. He served a two-year proselytizing mission for the LDS Church in Hungary. He studied at Cincinnati Christian University, earning an MDiv in Biblical Studies. He previously received a BBA from Thomas More University, from which he graduated summa cum laude. He has enjoyed a long career in the health insurance industry, and since 2019 has produced the podcast *Outer Brightness: From Mormon to Jesus*. He has been happily married to his best friend, Angela, for twenty-three years. They have five children, three dogs, and a grumpy old cat.

Chapter 7

Missionary Lesson Four: The Commandments

By Neal Humphrey

I didn't realize that I was vulnerable. I was about three-quarters of the way through my missionary service in the Midlands and Wales of Great Britain. My companion and I were canvassing (what we called "tracting") through a posh neighborhood of upper middle-class homes in Winsford, England. The homes were sturdy brick detached structures of individual houses, unlike the usual row houses or duplexes that were common in British towns. We were basically passing quickly down the street because nobody in a nice neighborhood like this one ever let us in. Whoever answered the door usually declined to talk to us, with varying degrees of politeness; occasionally someone would be rude.

I was vulnerable because I had completed our two-year missionary daily study plan in one year. Curiously, the study plan did not include reading through the Old Testament, so I focused my individual study time on the Old Testament. By the time we were tracting through the most prosperous neighborhood in Winsford, I had spent more than four hundred hours reading through the Old Testament. I had read it through twice, and then went back and studied various books and passages in detail. To say I was enthralled by Scripture would be an understatement. By the end of my mission, I had spent more than one thousand hours studying the Old Testament.

However, that study had led me to two unsettling conclusions. First, the culture of the Bible was not the same as the culture described in the Book of Mormon. The second conclusion was that some of our important proof texts for the validity of Mormon belief were serious misinterpretations of Scripture. It wouldn't be fair to describe my misgivings as a crisis of faith or, as Mormons would put it, losing my testimony. Rather, my skepticism was motivating me to study further. I certainly was not seeking an alternative to my membership in the Mormon Church.

Each house had a well-kept front yard – what the British call a "garden." My companion and I were dismissed by one resident, so we turned and walked to the next house. The next house had a low iron fence and a gate. The path to the front door consisted of a broad walk of bricks that had been laid in a herringbone pattern. We climbed the two steps into a broad alcove. The leaded windows on either side of the door were mostly screened by a pair of huge potted ferns. We rang the doorbell. In a neighborhood like this, all the doorbells worked.

After a moment, the door swung open and we were greeted by a well-groomed, young, thirty-something woman. She was dressed "tweedy," wearing brown flats, a tan wool skirt, and a blouse buttoned to the neck underneath a light green cardigan. We introduced ourselves, and to our surprise, she smiled and invited us in.

We were escorted to a parlor. Rugs covered a hardwood floor. The furniture was in the typical heavy British style. A few side stands were dustless and covered with small brass figurines, all of them polished to a high shine. A fireplace dominated one side of the parlor. Photos of the woman with family members cluttered the mantle. The room was comfortable, almost cozy.

We all sat down. My companion and I sat on a sofa, and the woman sat on an upholstered chair opposite us. We began our usual introductions and missionary presentation. She listened politely for a minute or two and then interrupted us. "You're the first Mormons I've met, and I have a few questions about your beliefs."

What we didn't know was that this woman was a theologically informed Christian, a member of the Church of England (Episcopal), and far better educated than the typical people who let us into their homes. We quickly lost control of the discussion as she probed us about what we believed.

For example, when we revealed that Mormons had additional scriptures such as the Book of Mormon, her reaction was, "So, you're like Muslims then? You have a certain regard for the Bible, which Muslims do, but like Muslims and the Qur'an, you have a preference for your Book of Mormon."

The only answer we had for that was "Yes."

She then insisted on getting a clear idea of our basic theology. What did we believe about God? We found ourselves asserting that we believed in the Father, Son, and Holy Ghost, but had to admit that we also believed they were one in purpose, yet were three different personages and not the one Triune God. This provoked her next question: "So who is your Creator God? Where did the universe come from?"

We couldn't answer the question because there is no systematic Mormon response as to the origin of the universe. The creation scene in the temple endowment ceremony makes it clear that Mormon gods organize existing matter into worlds. In the case of our world, the earth was the project of Michael (later the man Adam) and Jehovah at the command of another god named Elohim.

Not wanting to reveal this private Mormon doctrine to a non-member, I said, "Well, God has more knowledge than humans and can organize worlds in accordance with the laws of nature."

The woman's eyes widened. She stared at me for a moment and then said, "I would have rather thought that God created the laws of nature."

As I write this, I can look back fifty-three years and see that woman, hear her voice, and feel the shock that hit me with her statement. I realized then that my Mormon "god" was a puny entity compared to her Christian God. In addition, I knew she was describing the one true God who was captivating me as I read and studied the Old Testament.

There were a number of other incidents and milestones that finally led me out of Mormonism, but the Christian woman in the posh house in Winsford, England, produced the first and fatal damage that led to the erosion of my Mormon convictions.

Within three years after my mission, I became functionally inactive from the Mormon Church (although still holding a temple recommend). A dozen years after my mission, I received the sacrament of Christian baptism. A decade after my baptism, I graduated from seminary with a Master of Divinity degree and was ordained to Christian ministry as a Presbyterian pastor.

To this day, when people compliment me on my teaching or sermons, that comment is often punctuated by how they appreciate my Old Testament knowledge, the foundation of which was laid when I was a Mormon missionary.

The point of this preface is to alert the reader to the probability that Mormon missionaries are likely to have vulnerabilities – some reasonable skepticism about what they have been taught to believe. As you candidly present the gospel of Jesus Christ to Mormon missionaries, don't underestimate the potential of biblical truth to undermine their convictions.

As you have opportunity for such conversations, let me set forth two warnings.

First, Mormonism is fragile. There is no systematic theology. It is not difficult to present evidence of major changes and inconsistencies in Mormon Church doctrine, history, practices, and policies. Using such information in debate or confrontation with Mormon missionaries is non-productive. The missionaries will either retreat with a reinforced antagonism toward Christians, or they may accept the information, leave the Mormon Church, and live their lives as atheists or agnostics.

I don't know how many dozens of converts from Mormonism I have personally baptized. The process I used to teach the gospel to Mormons always focused on the positive. I would almost always use the assurance, "Here's how you can have a life after the ward" (the local Mormon congregation).

My purpose of this chapter is to offer enough information so that an encounter with Mormon missionaries will have the potential to build a relationship that will provoke the missionary into rethinking his or her beliefs.

Here is my second warning: care must be used with the Bible. Mormons are taught that the Bible has been corrupted, with many "plain and precious" teachings removed. A biblically based statement that conflicts with what a missionary believes is likely to be dismissed in favor of Latter-day revelation. There is some merit in taking the time to establish reasons to be confident in the Bible.

Commentary to the Fourth Lesson: The Commandments

Lesson 4 in *Preach My Gospel* is organized differently from the first three. The first three lessons explain the doctrinal foundation for how Mormons view the gospel of Jesus Christ, but

Lesson 4 explains specific commandments God has given that help Mormons apply gospel principles so they can live lives that are worthy of God's blessings.

The purpose of Lesson 4 is to teach or persuade potential converts to make themselves worthy of becoming Mormons. This is a critically important aspect of Mormon belief and life. A common phrase in Mormon exhortations is to "make yourself worthy" so that you can receive the Mormon priesthood, go to the temple, serve a mission, or hold an office in the Church. The list of what worthiness earns a Mormon is exhaustive.

If a person wants to become a Mormon, he has to prove that he is worthy. By contrast, there is an old and simple explanation that illustrates an important difference between Christianity and other religions. Simply stated, it is the difference between "do" and "done."

In non-Christian religion, the emphasis is almost always on what the adherents have to "do" in order to be redeemed or to have a relationship with the institution and whatever is worshiped as god. By contrast, true Christianity is primarily focused on what Christ alone has "done." This LDS missionary lesson is all about what Mormons have to do.

As a note, this lesson about following commandments is far more extensive than similar material from a few decades ago. Mormons have recognized that we are no longer in a Judeo-Christian culture where it can be presumed that people have a biblical understanding of right and wrong. This lesson presents the details in a way that a potential convert will know what constitutes how to be worthy enough to become a Mormon.

On the surface, there is nothing wrong with helping people live a biblically based ethical and moral lifestyle. Millions of Mormons strive to do so and live healthy and productive lives. For my own part, I still live the kind of life I was taught to live when I was a young Mormon. Therefore, it would be silly to argue against obeying God's commandments. The issue with LDS teaching is their extrabiblical commandments as well as a misrepresentation of the doctrine of salvation by faith.

In Mormonism, the pressure to be worthy can be toxic. For some Mormons, striving to be worthy leads to neurotic perfectionism with symptoms of depression, suicidal ideation, eating disorders, poor health, and constant fear of failure. Because of this, Utah often leads the nation in the use of antidepressant drugs.[88] The leading cause of death for young men in Utah between the ages of fifteen and twenty-five is suicide.[89] When the Utah media reports on these unfortunate facts, there is always some comment on the social pressure exerted by the Mormon Church.

Moreover, failing to keep oneself worthy from a Mormon perspective will have punitive consequences. As a personal example, I am the eldest of five children. All of us were worthy of being married in Mormon temples. Our mother was not worthy because she was addicted to nicotine and was barred by Mormon leaders from attending the weddings of each of her five children. Years later, I asked each of my siblings how they felt about our mother being banned from our weddings. Almost word for word, they each answered, "It was her own fault." My mother couldn't "do" what Mormons were supposed to do.

By contrast, when I have shared this anecdote with Christians, they were outraged. This is an example of how potential converts often have no idea what they are getting into if they join the Mormon Church.

To repeat a previous point, Christianity is first focused on Christ's sacrificial death on the cross. This is the functional definition of the Christian doctrine of grace. Our relationship with God is a gift given freely to sinners through the sacrificial

88 Julie Cart, "Study Finds Utah Leads Nation in Antidepressant Use," *Los Angeles Times*, February 20, 2022, https://www.latimes.com/archives/la-xpm-2002-feb-20-mn-28924-story.html.

89 "Utah Deaths by Age and Gender," World Life Expectancy, December 22, 2021, https://www.worldlifeexpectancy.com/utah-cause-of-death-by-age-and-gender.

work of Christ. Sinners cannot earn salvation by making themselves worthy outside of Christ.

You will note that the word "grace" does not appear at all in this lesson on commandments. How Mormons view grace is revealed at the end of the previous LDS lesson, where grace is inaccurately and outrageously redefined as power bestowed by their god so a Mormon can keep the commandments and do good works to make themselves worthy.[90]

This fourth lesson on keeping commandments is critically important because if a missionary fails to get a commitment from a potential convert to follow the commandments, there will be no baptism – no "sale," so to speak. In my mission during the 1960s, our administrative handbook was explicit: the only measure of a successful mission was convert baptisms. Fifty years later, that criterion may have softened somewhat, but there is no doubt that effective missionaries are those who bring converts into the Mormon Church.

Obedience

In every section of Lesson 4, there are instructions to offer "invitations" – to ask for commitment to some principle. The first is to "obey the laws of God." Curiously, this invitation takes place before the missionary reveals what Mormons believe the laws of God are.

Pray Often

The next invitation is to pray. The missionaries will instruct a potential convert that prayer usually has to be done while kneeling. Not described in the lesson are the rest of the Mormon prayer postures of folding arms, bowing heads, and closing eyes.

---

90   *Preach My Gospel*, 70.

This gives rise to obvious questions about the limits of prayer postures. Why not be biblical? For example, why not lift your eyes to heaven? Why not raise your hands?

Study the "Scriptures"

The next invitation is to read scripture every day. The four Mormon "standard works" are the Book of Mormon, the Doctrine and Covenants, the Pearl of Great Price, and the Bible. Most of the scriptural citations supporting the invitation to pray are from the Book of Mormon. The lesson intentionally redirects a potential convert's attention away from the Bible and toward the Mormon "scriptures." It includes a list of nine citations to guide a potential convert in their prayers. Four are from the Book of Mormon, four are from the Doctrine and Covenants, and one is from the Bible. The biblical text is 1 Kings 19:11-12, where God speaks to Elijah in *a still small voice*.

The challenge that could be offered to a missionary at this point is to ask, "What is so dangerous about reading the Bible?" It could initiate an interesting discussion.

Keep the Sabbath Day Holy

The next section is Sabbath keeping, which is among the several visible marks of a Mormon's zeal. With the exception of some occupations, Mormons do not work on Sunday, nor do they recreate or play. They dress in their Sunday best and leave those clothes on all day. This practice might be stifling for some, but it works for many.

My next-door neighbors are active Mormons and are very nice people with a huge family. One day, the mother told me that she had a cascade of dirty laundry that had to be dealt with. She decided to run a few loads on Sunday. When her washing machine broke down, she ruefully admitted, with some good humor, that her god was punishing her for breaking the Sabbath.

In keeping with obeying commandments to make yourself worthy, the invitation on page 78 of *PMG* includes: "Will you prepare yourself to partake of the sacrament worthily?" This is curious since "worthy" has not been defined.

By the way, in Mormon-speak, the word "sacrament" is only used to describe the Mormon version of the Eucharist or Lord's Table. The elements Mormons serve in their sacrament are white bread and water, which, when you think about it, makes perfect sense given their watered-down Christology.

Even though the missionaries have revealed only a small portion of the necessary commandments converts will have to follow, the lesson plan at this point allows for an invitation to be baptized and join the Mormon Church. This system of lessons is like all the versions of missionary lessons since the 1960s, with its emphasis on "closing the sale," or getting a baptized convert. If this were an honest sales manual, this early invitation to be baptized and join the Mormon Church would be called a "test close" – a probe to see what else must be taught in order to persuade the person to make a commitment.

The next section is where things really start to get interesting.

Follow the Prophet

Typical of the unique Mormon beliefs, the Mormon teaching about prophets is distant and distorted from what the Bible teaches.

I explained in my preface that I spent hundreds of hours during the last half of my Mormon mission reading and studying the Old Testament. Imagine my surprise when I encountered the narrative in 2 Kings 22 and repeated in 2 Chronicles 34. Those chapters describe that the Book of the Law was discovered during a remodel of the temple. The temple officials took the book to King Josiah and read it to him. The king and his advisers realized that they had a compliance problem, so they decided to consult their prophet to see what the Lord had to say about their situation.

The prophetess was Huldah. I was shocked to read that she was the wife of a tailor who managed the royal wardrobe. The biblical report of a woman prophet rocked the foundations of my Mormon beliefs. And Huldah prophesied. The result was a revival in Judah. Moreover, many Bible scholars believe that among the benefits of the revival was the assembly of seven books of the Bible (Deuteronomy, Judges, Joshua, 1 and 2 Samuel, and 1 and 2 Kings) in the form we have them today. The woman prophet Huldah was a powerful and historic voice of God.

The New Testament refers to seven contemporary prophets. Some consider John the Baptist to be the last of the Old Testament prophets. The book of Acts reports five other individual prophets. Agabus was among the prophets of the early Christian church (Acts 11:27-28; 21:10-11). However, the New Testament reports more women prophets than men. Anna the prophetess was among the first to recognize the infant Jesus as the Messiah (Luke 2:36-38). Philip the deacon had four daughters who are described as prophetesses (Acts 21:8-9).

These men and women called by God to be prophets were never institutional leaders. In fact, no biblical prophet was the leader of a kingdom or church. God calls prophets to proclaim His Word and will from the margins of institutions.

Moreover, the office of prophet as defined by the Bible continued in the early church. Even today, the office of prophet is recognized among charismatic Christian groups. The true church of Jesus Christ does have men and women who were called by God to be prophets, which can be a shock for Mormon missionaries.

God calling women to be prophets can be an interesting challenge for Mormon women. I have used this biblical illustration in teaching women during their transition out of the Mormon Church, and they have reported that it was very helpful. Keeping in mind these days the biblical reality of women prophets is important because there is a likelihood that the missionaries whom the reader encounters will be women – known to Mormons as "sister missionaries." When I was a Mormon missionary in the late 1960s, my mission had about two hundred missionaries. Only eight were women. That is less than 5 percent. I have recently spoken with returned missionaries and elders who are currently in service who consistently report that more than 20 percent of the Mormon missionary force consists of women.

Mormon missionaries are likely to challenge someone with the question: "Do you have a prophet of God at the head of your church?" The Christian answer is, "Of course not."

By contrast, Mormon prophets are institutional leaders who must be followed. A potential convert is required to make a commitment to follow the Mormon prophet.

In early Mormonism, it took a while before Joseph Smith was acknowledged as head of the Church. The first presiding bishop, Edward Partridge, assumed he was the leader of the newly organized Mormon Church. He presumed that Mormon ecclesiology (church organization) would be similar to many Christian denominations in which bishops were the leaders.[91] However, the role of prophet in Mormon leadership quickly evolved into an authoritarian model that has no parallel among Christian churches. An example of the exalted role of Mormon prophets is illustrated in the first and third lines of the refrain to the popular Mormon hymn, "Praise to the Man":

> Hail to the Prophet, ascended to heaven! . . .
> Mingling with Gods, he can plan for his brethren.[92]

---

91   Dale Beecher, "The Office of Bishop," *Dialogue: A Journal of Mormon Thought* 15, no. 4 (Winter 1982), 103.

92   "Praise to the Man," *Hymns of the Church of Jesus Christ of Latter-day Saints* (Salt Lake City: Deseret Book, 1985), 27-28.

Tossing this information from the hymn's refrain into a conversation with Mormon missionaries can open up an enlightening conversation about the role of Mormon prophets and, not incidentally, their doctrine of plurality of gods.

Finally, are the Mormon prophets frauds? Of course they are. Anyone can make a quick search of the internet and find dozens of documented false prophecies by Joseph Smith and Brigham Young. The purpose of this section isn't so much to demonstrate that Mormon prophets are false, but that the very premise of prophetic leadership is false.

Still, I can't resist reporting my favorite false prophecy uttered by Joseph Smith. My great-great-great grandfather was the Mormon leader and pioneer Anson Call. If you do not know what Anson Call was supposed to be famous for, then Joseph Smith is a false prophet.

Here is an excerpt from my great-great-great-grandfather's diary, dated April 6, 1842, in which Anson Call tells what Joseph Smith revealed:

> There are some of these standing here that will perform a great work in that land [the Rocky Mountains]. . . . There is Anson, he shall go and assist in building cities from one end of the country to the other and you shall perform as great a work as has ever been done by man, and the nations of the earth shall be astonished and many of them will be gathered in that land and assist in building cities."

Sorry, Granddad. Establishing the town of Fillmore, Utah, and later Call's Fort with your brothers Omer and Homer, does not fulfill the prophecy of "building cities from one end of the country to the other."

The Ten Commandments

It is useful to make it clear to missionaries that you have a functional knowledge of Mormonism. You may have some formal training in the Bible, Christian church history, and theology, but Mormon missionaries' knowledge of even their own tradition is likely to be sketchy, and what they know about Christianity will be less, and likely distorted. With this in mind, be cautious not to overwhelm missionaries by uncharitably exposing their ignorance. Discussing the Ten Commandments affords an opportunity to be both gracious and informative.

First of all, a close examination of Exodus 20:2-17 and Deuteronomy 5:6-21 will reveal that there are possibly fourteen commandments. So why do official lists have ten? Because the Bible says so: *[God] declared to you His covenant which He commanded you to perform, the Ten Commandments* (Deuteronomy 4:13). As a result, different traditions sort out the fourteen imperatives into different lists of the Ten Commandments. The three primary variations are found in Judaism, Catholicism, and Orthodoxy/Protestantism. For example, Sabbath keeping is number three on the Catholic list, but number four on the Jewish and Protestant/Orthodox list.

The different numbering used by different traditions doesn't change the impact or meaning of the Ten Commandments, but it does raise a question that can be posed to Mormon missionaries. Why do Mormons use the Protestant list? The Ten Commandments are found in the Book of Mormon,[93] but that context doesn't suggest an arrangement. The Ten Commandments in the missionaries' lesson plan uses Exodus 20 for reference and is Protestant.

It is always fun when teaching from the law of Moses to remind people that there aren't just ten commandments, but there are 613 commandments. We all break dozens of those

---

93   Mosiah 12:34-36; 13:15-16; 13:21-24 (Book of Mormon).

commandments just about every day – from eating bacon to wearing clothing woven with blended fabrics. A point you can make with missionaries is to remind them that the law of Moses and the Old Testament gave rise to the most durable religious and ethnic group in human history: the Jews. This historical fact affirms that the Bible alone is sufficient for teaching God's children how to live their lives to the full in faith and service.

The purpose of this type of discussion with the missionaries is simply to show them how interesting a deep study of the Bible can be. It would be entirely appropriate to warn them: "Studying the Bible will change your life."

The invitation at the end of this section of *Preach My Gospel* is, "Will you keep the Ten Commandments?" Please do.

Live the Law of Chastity

Chastity is defined by Mormons as limiting sexual relations to those between a man and a woman in a legal, monogamous marriage. Period. This section also teaches that all single people, including those with same-sex attractions, are to be celibate. Exclusive and binary relationships are scriptural and this is in alignment with what Christians also believe.

While it pops up as a non sequitur, the lesson also teaches against abortion. While this is also in alignment with Christian beliefs, it does raise an opportunity to ask, "*Why* is abortion wrong?" In response, a missionary might be evasive, perhaps relying on typical arguments about the rights of the unborn. An enlightening discussion, however, will arise if a missionary will admit that there are "spirits" in the preexistence, born of heavenly mothers. These preexistent spirits need to be born of human mothers on earth so they can live a life and undergo a period of mortal probation and testing. A mortal life is the only path to proving oneself worthy of eternally progressing to

celestial glory and godhood. Abortion would obviously termi-
nate those spirits' opportunity, and that is the primary reason
for the Mormon objection to abortion.

There is an inconsistency in Mormon belief when it comes to
the tragedy of the deaths of young children. If a child dies before
the age of eight, which is the "age of accountability" in Mormon
belief, that child goes straight to the highest Mormon heaven. There
they wait for their survivors to do the necessary temple work so
the dead child can eternally progress to exaltation. This belief is
a comfort to grieving parents and relatives. If it weren't for the
temple work, this would be close to grace. A couple of uncomfortable questions for missionaries would be, "Do you do temple work
for aborted children?" "Do the spirits of aborted children return
to the preexistence and get back in line for a chance to be born?"

This conversation about preexistent spirits could give rise
to other interesting questions: "Are there mothers in heaven?"
(Answer, "Yes.") "Do these mothers in heaven give birth to all
the billions and billions of spirit children?" (Answer, "Yes.")
"Are there fathers in heaven?" (Answer, "Just one.") "So there
is polygamy in heaven?" (Answer, "Yes.")

If a missionary will disclose these private beliefs, it is a sign
of progress toward a relationship based on candor and honesty.

Part of the challenge for missionaries in regard to this lesson is that they are required to ask some intrusive questions
of their investigators about sexual practices. I imagine there
have been people wondering what business it is of a kid half
their age to want to know what's going on in their bedrooms.
Still, missionaries have to determine if people are cohabiting,
and if so, they must insist that they either get married or secure
separate residences before being baptized. The instructions even
include excluding polygamists.

If there is a serious problem, such as a woman who has had
an abortion or someone who is a practicing homosexual, the

missionary is instructed to set up a special screening "interview" with the mission president.

In the Mormon culture, the word "interview" has special meaning. A Mormon who is being interviewed by a leader is often facing a rebuke for some shortcoming. Other occasions when interviews are required to determine worthiness include priesthood advancement, baptism, temple recommends, and preparedness for a church position. Sometimes Mormons will request an interview, or a counseling session, with a leader.

With this insight in mind, if a Christian's relationship with missionaries continues for too long and is beginning to influence them, they expose themselves to the possibility of being called in for an interview with their mission president, which might turn out to be a punitive experience. Then there is a good chance that they will be transferred to a different district.

Obey the Word of Wisdom

The Word of Wisdom is the Mormon dietary code that exhorts members to be moderate in the consumption of meat (which is largely ignored) and to not use or consume alcoholic beverages, tobacco, tea, and coffee. On the face of it, there's nothing wrong with having a dietary code, but at the same time, such codes can also lead to abuse and hypocrisy.

The Word of Wisdom, found in Doctrine and Covenants 89, supposedly began as advice in a revelation to Joseph Smith and was loosely followed for decades. By 1921, however, it was reinterpreted as a rigid commandment. A Mormon who couldn't follow the Word of Wisdom would be considered unworthy of priesthood advancement or of receiving a temple recommend. Moreover, as *PMG* states on page 81, Mormons believe that "People who obey the Word of Wisdom are more receptive to spiritual truths."

It has been interesting to observe Mormons as they relate to the Word of Wisdom. One evening there was an unfortunate crash of a propane tanker about a mile north of my church in Utah. Emergency responders were concerned about the possibility of an explosion that could level an area a half mile in diameter, so hundreds of residences were evacuated. Three of the locations for evacuees were my church, the LDS meetinghouse across the street, and our town's city hall next door. We took care of people all night.

One of the community leaders, a devout Mormon, quipped later that "If you needed your caffeine hot that night, it was being served at the Presbyterian church."

A few years later, I was at a weeklong training event for Boy Scout leaders. There were only two non-Mormons in attendance, so I brought my own coffee and brewing gear. The Mormons brought a stack of cases of Mountain Dew, a beverage with one of the highest caffeine contents of all soft drinks. This explains the amusing Mormon saying, "You can tell the piety of a Church member by the temperature at which they consume their caffeine." Yes, Mormons have a sense of humor.

Again, there's nothing wrong with the wisdom of a dietary code. When I was an active Mormon (and for years after I lapsed), I continued to adhere to the Word of Wisdom. However, to use such a code for social control is another matter altogether. If Mormons do not obey the Word of Wisdom:

- They cannot serve on a mission.

- They cannot become an elder (or receive any other priesthood advancement).

- They cannot get married in the temple.

- They cannot renew their temple recommend.

- They cannot be called to important Church positions such as bishop or stake president.

- They cannot consider themselves to be faithful Mormons.

The Presbyterian church I served at in Utah provided space for eight twelve-step recovery groups, most of them serving drug addicts or alcoholics. Almost all of the more than one hundred attendees were from a Mormon background, although none were active Mormons. While there are Mormons who are trying to provide a constructive response to the many in their membership who struggle with addictions, thus far the bottom line is still punitive.

One of the more disturbing elements of *PMG*, Lesson 4, is an "Overcoming Addictions" section on page 82. The lesson advises missionaries to refer people with an addictive substance-abuse problem to a Mormon recovery program website. Unfortunately, it still offers an eight-step counseling plan for missionaries to use with people who have difficulty observing the Word of Wisdom. Missionaries are even permitted to counsel addicts. So without a lick of professional training, missionaries are allowed to initiate an intervention that they are manifestly unqualified to perform.

There are two points in regard to this. First, counseling in matters for which missionaries or lay ward and stake leaders have no training or qualifications is a serious problem in Mormonism. Whether it is dealing with addiction, a distressed marriage, abuse, or even financial advice, missionaries and Mormon leaders are simply not equipped. Second, this willingness of Mormons to intervene where they should not arises from the conviction that their priesthood power gives them the authority to step into situations that even a professionally trained counselor would enter cautiously.

In an encounter with missionaries, this provides an opportunity to ask a reasonable, if challenging, question: "Do you really think you are prepared to constructively help someone who is caught up in addiction?" The purpose of a question like this is to help missionaries see that their Mormon leaders have not prepared them for some of the circumstances they will be facing.

In encounters with missionaries, there is a high probability that someone close to them, such as a parent, sibling, close relative, or friend, has been on the receiving end of some Mormon leader's judgment because of the Word of Wisdom. If that circumstance can be uncovered, then you may have a chance to illuminate how unreasonable, unfair, or even unrighteous such a judgment has been.

Finally, if the missionaries are willing to accept the teachings of Jesus on the matter of dietary codes, they can be reminded that Jesus clarified such restrictions. What a person consumes doesn't make them unworthy.

> So [Jesus] said to them, "Are you thus without understanding also? Do you not perceive that whatever enters a man from outside cannot defile him, because it does not enter his heart but his stomach, and is eliminated, thus purifying all foods?" And He said, "What comes out of a man, that defiles a man. For from within, out of the heart of men, proceed evil thoughts, adulteries, fornications, murders, thefts, covetousness, wickedness, deceit, lewdness, an evil eye, blasphemy, pride, foolishness. All these evil things come from within and defile a man." (Mark 7:18-23)

I will conclude with a brief story. Several years ago, I was being interviewed by a pastor-search team. One of the women on the panel surprised me with the question, "How do you feel about beer and brewing beer?" What I didn't know was that her husband was an award-winning amateur brewer.

Wondering where the question was taking me, I asked for a copy of their pew Bible. As I turned to Deuteronomy, I explained that one of the three tithes in the law of Moses was a "festival tithe," in which a tenth of the increase from one's ranch or farm was brought to the one place to which the Lord God had called everyone. The purpose was to worship God and have a huge potluck feast. Then I read:

> *But if the journey is too long for you, so that you*
> *are not able to carry the tithe, or if the place where*
> *the Lord your God chooses to put His name is too*
> *far from you, when the Lord your God has blessed*
> *you, then you shall exchange it for money, take the*
> *money in your hand, and go to the place which the*
> *Lord your God chooses. And you shall spend that*
> *money for whatever your heart desires: for oxen*
> *or sheep, for wine or similar drink, for whatever*
> *your heart desires; you shall eat there before the*
> *Lord your God, and you shall rejoice, you and your*
> *household. (Deuteronomy 14:24-26)*

It was reported to me later that this was the moment that crystallized the search team's decision to call me as their pastor. Of course, Scripture does warn us not to be drunk with wine (Ephesians 5:18), and some people, for various acceptable reasons, may choose to abstain from alcohol. This is simply to say that alcohol in and of itself is not forbidden in Scripture, and strict rules requiring total abstinence are generally extrabiblical commandments.

This anecdote leads to the next topic in the missionary lessons.

Keep the Law of Tithing

As I just mentioned, there were three tithes in the Law: the festival tithe, a tithe for the Lord (Leviticus 27:30 and elsewhere), and a charity tithe to be paid every third year for the support of Levites, widows, and orphans (Deuteronomy 26:12). That is an annual total of 23.3 percent, but there were no government taxes. Besides, the Israelites consumed the festival tithe.

My point is that the tithe is certainly biblical. However, while the New Testament encourages offerings, the word "tithe" is never used. While a tithe is a tenth, the only giving percentages ever mentioned in the New Testament are 50 percent in the case of Zacchaeus (Luke 19:8), and 100 percent in the case of the rich young ruler (Matthew 19:16-29; Mark 10:17-30; Luke 18:18-30), which makes 10 percent look pretty reasonable.

An important New Testament principle is that any offering for the work of the kingdom of God should be a *cheerful* act (2 Corinthians 9:7).

I learned the principle of the tithe as a Mormon, and I still practice the discipline, which God uses to bless my local church. Most people with decent jobs who know how to prudently manage their personal finances can afford the tithe. In my case, prudently managing my money includes driving a twenty-year-old pickup truck that I bought used. Upkeep on that truck is still less expensive than new vehicle payments.

Mormons rarely, if ever, use the word "tithe." Rather, they have come to prefer "tithing" as both a noun and a verb, which I will do for the rest of this section.

First, the Mormon Church is incredibly rich. Their liquid assets for church operations are about a billion dollars. Annual revenue from tithing amounts to seven billion dollars, all of which goes directly to Church headquarters in Salt Lake City.[94] The irony is that

---

94 For an example, see Tony Semerad, "Here's a deeper look at how the LDS Church makes its billions," *Salt Lake Tribune*, September 27, 2021.

the tithing revenue stream could stop completely and the Church could continue to fund all its operations on investment income alone. Moreover, the Mormon Church has numerous secular business ventures outside of their nonprofit church operations, which are also valued at a billion dollars. On a per member basis, the Mormon Church is the wealthiest religious body on the planet.

Mormons take the principle of tithing seriously. To be a Mormon in full faith and fellowship, paying a full tithe is required. In fact, near the end of the calendar year, ward bishops will start to schedule "Tithing Declaration" interviews. Every member of the ward is expected to meet with the local bishop and review their contributions to make sure they have paid their full tenth.

Folk tales abound about Mormon bishops requiring bank statements or tax returns during tithing interviews to confirm that a member is contributing the full necessary tenth. While these are probably apocryphal, it could be fun to ask missionaries what kind of documentation a Church member has to bring to the tithing declaration interview.

Still, if Mormons fail to pay a full tithe, they will expose themselves to the same list of sanctions that are imposed on those who do not obey the Word of Wisdom.

The lesson also contains a misdirection when it claims, "Tithing does not pay local Church leaders, who serve voluntarily without receiving payment of any kind."[95] That is true. What is not disclosed, though, is that General Authorities who lead the Mormon Church are all paid top executive salaries, most of them in seven figures. While missionaries will likely hold with the usual Mormon prejudices against Christian clergy because they get paid, it is unlikely that they will be aware of the millions of dollars that their top leaders are paid. A challenging question would be to ask why the salaries of General Authorities are not mentioned.

---

95   *Preach My Gospel*, 83.

Observe the Law of the Fast

The Law of the Fast is a unique and charming feature of Mormon life. First, by "fast," Mormons mean a deprivation fast of no food or beverages for a specified time. Most Christians are in traditions where selective fasts are part of holy seasons and days where alcohol and/or meat are avoided. Selective fasting is unknown to Mormons.

Individual Mormons will put out a call for prayer and fasting during a family crisis. My wife and I still receive such petitions from our extended family and will participate on behalf of someone in the hospital or who is in some other sort of difficulty.

The fast mentioned in this lesson is a discipline in which Mormons monthly skip two meals, then donate the cost of those meals to a special fund that supports the Mormon Church welfare system. It is called the "fast offering." On the first Sunday of the month, Mormon boys and teenagers visit all the households in the ward to collect the offering (some members make a direct donation). The theory is that the welfare system can operate without adding the burden of a special offering to meet the needs of the poor. It works. The Mormon welfare system is vast, efficient, and largely funded by the fast offering.

Obey and Honor the Law

This section makes an obvious point. The missionaries want to attract law-abiding citizens to their church. If a potential convert has a criminal record or is on probation/parole, then the missionaries have to refer them to their mission president for further vetting (the "interview").

I live in an urban county with more than 360,000 residents. It is the third largest county in the state of Utah. Some years ago, I spent a year on a citizen's review panel studying the merits of expanding our county jail and how to fund it. It turned out to be a critical need, and the citizens of the county voted to approve our recommendation to fund the expansion with a bond issue. One of the things I learned during that study was that the rate and types of crime committed in our county were typical of an American community of our size and racial-economic profile. At the time, about 80 percent of the population was Mormon. In other words, Mormons are just as prone as other communities to have a minority of people who do not obey the law.

One aspect in which Utah is unique, however, is affinity fraud. Affinity fraud is a crime that uses relationships, often in a church setting, to promote pyramid or Ponzi schemes that rob gullible people of their "investments." Utah is the affinity-fraud capital of America.

While it is fair to say that Mormons want to be good, law-abiding citizens, their community basically has the same mixed results as everywhere else.

Bottom Line

Again, exhorting a religious community to follow God's commandments is not a bad thing. However, enforcing compliance to extrabiblical commandments to keep people in line with what amounts to a judgmental bludgeon is evil.

Hopefully, an encounter with missionaries in the context of this lesson will teach the missionaries to ask these kinds of questions when Mormon leaders try to impose compliance with extrabiblical Mormon commandments. Is it fair? Is it healthy? Who benefits from such compliance?

Going back to my encounter with the Anglican churchwoman in Winsford, England, she was an informed Christian of conviction, incisive in her discourse with me, and not the least bit confrontational or combative. God used her to successfully initiate the most unexpected and blessed transformation of my life.

* * * *

Neal Humphrey grew up as a sixth-generation Mormon, a descendant of the early Utah pioneers. He served an LDS mission from 1966-1968 in the Central British Mission. Humphrey attended Brigham Young University and was married in the Los Angeles temple. He left Mormonism to follow Christ. He earned a Master of Divinity degree from San Francisco Theological Seminary and is an ordained minister. He has pastored several churches, from Presbyterian to Baptist. Rev. Humphrey is an avid fly fishermen and snow skier, and he also enjoys cooking, hiking, camping, and dogs.

Chapter 8

Missionary Lesson Five:
Laws and Ordinances

By Michael Flournoy

"You're the torchbearer." My grandpa's words echoed through my mind. I pictured his misty eyes as he gripped my shoulder. I was a seventh generation Latter-day Saint. Many people in my maternal line had gone to preach the restored gospel and had miraculous experiences. I would be the first to serve a mission on my father's side. It was my duty to set a good example for my brothers so they would serve missions as well. It all hinged on me.

Yet suddenly my testimony was reeling from an encounter I just had with an evangelical Christian. I just spent three hours on the defensive, enduring arguments I never thought existed. Worst of all, the evangelical's weapon of choice was the Bible.

I was dumbfounded. I thought the Bible was supposed to be on my side, yet it repeatedly sided with my opponent. How could that be? We were the restored Church. It was a Church my ancestors had been persecuted for, crossed the plains in handcarts to preserve, and even died for. The legacy of my entire family hinged on the LDS Church being what it claimed to be. Could it really all be a lie?

I felt as if someone had pounded me in the stomach with a wrecking ball. I couldn't even imagine a life outside of Mormonism. My faith was an integral part of my being; anything else was an unfathomable nightmare filled with damnation, darkness, and misery from which I could never awaken.

Crossing the Threshold

A lot happened after that fateful encounter in 2003. God used my meeting with an evangelical named Ed Enochs to plant a seed of truth in my heart. I realized that the Bible was God's Word and that it was a reliable source to use to search for answers.

At the start of my truth journey, the biblical text seemed to support my LDS faith. Enthused by this, I became an amateur apologist whose goal was to protect unsuspecting Mormons from the onslaught of evangelicals. I spent countless hours debating Christians online, and in 2012, I wrote a book entitled *A Biblical Defense of Mormonism.*

The book drew the attention of local Latter-day Saints, and I was invited to do presentations on how to defend the faith with the Bible. Evangelicals also reached out and offered to debate me publicly. I was obsessed with proving that Mormonism was true. I debated everyone I could and was constantly thinking of new ways around Christian arguments.

In 2015, I decided to go after the crown jewel of Christianity. I started a serious study on the topic of grace, knowing that if I could disprove the notion of salvation by faith alone, then Protestant Christianity would collapse.

I discovered that grace in the Bible was different from how the LDS Church described it. It was not merely enabling power, but it was salvific power. I realized that Christians were justified freely because Christ gave us His righteousness when we believed in Him.

Within a year, I left the LDS Church. Grace won me over. It was the antidote to a lifetime of works-based religion. My trust and my life now belonged to Jesus alone. Based on my experience, I believe that grace is the best weapon in our arsenal when the Mormon missionaries come knocking.

Another Gospel

Lesson 5 in *Preach My Gospel* is about laws and ordinances. It teaches about the various organizations in the LDS Church and about the importance of priesthood authority to provide saving ordinances. The chapter goes into depth about what good members of the Church should be doing, which includes missionary work, serving the community, getting married in the temple for time and all eternity, and faithfully observing and recording family history so those who have passed on can receive these ordinances vicariously.

Lesson 5 is actually meant for new members who have already been baptized into the LDS Church. With an "investigator," the missionaries probably won't go into too much detail on most of these topics. After all, why does an outsider need to know about the Church's organizations, structure, and procedures?

However, *PMG* encourages missionaries to be flexible with what they teach and when. One topic that is heavily emphasized throughout the chapter is priesthood authority, and the missionaries may try to sneak it in after they have exhausted other talking points, or it could rear its head on the first visit. Either way, it is the perfect opportunity to share the gospel of grace, as I will explain later.

Let me give two general pieces of advice before we begin. First, I recommend embracing the role of an investigator who is taking the journey of truth with them. This doesn't mean denying your faith or acting as if you don't hold strong convictions, but it puts you on their level and makes them more interested in hearing your side of the story. When you come across as a know-it-all who is trying to save them, you are likely to scare them off. I approach LDS missionaries the way I would approach a stray cat. You have to put them at ease and show that you are not a threat.

Second, be aware that Mormons hold many different viewpoints. Some believe strongly in grace, thinking that we only need to enter into a baptismal covenant and that God will overlook our sins. Others believe they have to end all sinful behavior to be worthy, but they may need centuries or more to achieve that goal in the next life.

If confronted directly, the elders will claim that theirs is a gospel of grace. Do not be deceived. As a missionary, I was trained to avoid direct attacks on people's beliefs, but to find common ground instead. I didn't even know I was being deceptive or was teaching a different gospel. I just thought I was building onto what people already believed. Mormons are adept at using Protestant language and lacing it with heresy.

Finally, realize that the missionaries are just young men and women. They are not hardened apologists for the faith. They are victims of a mind-control cult, and we must keep that in mind. They are not our enemies. Some of them, like me, were born into the faith and are simply Mormon because they have never known an alternative.

Just be sure that you do not mistake the Mormon gospel for the biblical gospel. *PMG* states, "Work with members to help people you are teaching accept and begin living these laws and ordinances. Help people recognize that by keeping God's laws, they will retain a remission of their sins and stay on the pathway to exaltation."[96]

---

96   *Preach My Gospel*, 86.

This is not the gospel of grace, which tells us that Christ justifies the ungodly by imputing His righteousness to them. Imputation refers to the biblical truth that Jesus lived a perfect life of obedience on our behalf and offered it to us on the cross, contingent on nothing but faith. In contrast, Mormonism is a gospel of works. It is a religion that teaches that with God's help, we can be perfect. Grace is reduced to an enabling power, but salvation is gained from obedience and repentance from sin. Mormon scripture actually states that "it is by grace that we are saved, after all we can do."[97]

Ultimately, the LDS Church rejects imputation and teaches a gospel of amputation instead. That is, man must amputate the sin from his life in order to become worthy. Two attributes of this false gospel are as follows: (1) Since obedience and repentance make us worthy, sin can undo salvation, and (2) a special priesthood authority is required to perform saving ordinances.

Mormonism is not unique, for every religion on earth is built the same way. Man must do something to merit salvation, and only his particular religious organization provides the means necessary to do it. This is why the LDS Church doesn't recognize anyone's baptism unless it was done by someone holding priesthood authority.

Chapter 5 of *PMG* poses a laundry list of things we need to do to live out "the gospel," including missionary work, marriage, genealogy, temple work, serving our fellow man and the Church, and teaching one another. In addition to all this, we must endure to the end. This gospel never offers any assurance or affords any point when someone can rest in the grace of Christ. Because of that, it is not good news at all. As we go through each point, I will explain how the individual teachings of *PMG* affect the lives of Latter-day Saints, leaving them hopeless and in desperate need of the gospel of Jesus Christ.

---

97   2 Nephi 25:23 (Book of Mormon).

Priesthood Authority

The *PMG* manual has this to say about priesthood authority: "Priesthood is the power and authority given to man to act in God's name for the salvation of his children. Priesthood power blesses all of us. Through the priesthood, women and men receive the ordinances of salvation, as well as the blessings of healing, comfort, and counsel."[98]

The missionaries will claim that God gave Joseph Smith priesthood authority when he restored the Church, and that this authority has been passed down since then from generation to generation. In their eyes, priesthood is what makes a contract binding. A baptism or covenant doesn't count if the priesthood is not involved. Marriages cannot continue into the next life if they are not sealed with the priesthood. The fifth point in the LDS Articles of Faith says, "We believe that a man must be called of God, by prophecy, and by the laying on of hands by those who are in authority, to preach the gospel and administer in the ordinances thereof."[99]

This principle immediately grants all authority to the heads of the LDS Church – the prophet and apostles. No one can use the priesthood, even if it has been conferred to them, unless its use has been delegated by a higher-ranking member of the Church. No one can decide what the doctrine of the Church is either. Everything is dictated by the men at the top. In the face of prophetic revelation, scripture and personal revelation play second fiddle. Those who rank above you in the Church even have authority to receive revelation for your life.

Priesthood is a stumbling block for many Mormons. They cannot even conceive of becoming Christian, and they will ask, "Where is your authority? Where are your prophets and

---

98   *Preach My Gospel*, 87.
99   Articles of Faith 5 (Pearl of Great Price).

apostles?" It seems obvious to them that we are not the church that Jesus established in the New Testament.

Priesthood is the glue that holds Mormonism together, yet priesthood is also Mormonism's Achilles' heel. While priesthood authority sounds great on the surface, the concept raises significant problems. For example, it is only for men, to the exclusion of women. This automatically puts a divide between the genders, whereas Christians believe in a priesthood of all believers – that both men and women can go to God through Jesus Christ (1 Peter 2:4-5, 9). As a man growing up in the Mormon Church, I realized that priesthood was a heavy burden to carry. Doctrine and Covenants 121:36-37 states:

> That the rights of the priesthood are inseparably connected with the powers of heaven, and that the powers of heaven cannot be controlled nor handled only upon the principles of righteousness. That they may be conferred upon us, it is true; but when we undertake to cover our sins, or to gratify our pride, our vain ambition, or to exercise control or dominion or compulsion upon the souls of the children of men, in any degree of unrighteousness, behold, the heavens withdraw themselves; the Spirit of the Lord is grieved; and when it is withdrawn, Amen to the priesthood or the authority of that man.

Even from a young age, I was acutely aware of my sins. In Mormon culture, everyone dresses nice on Sundays and pretends to be worthy. I got the impression that I alone struggled to keep the commandments. The Doctrine and Covenants said that if I was unrighteous to any degree, my priesthood authority would end. I was sometimes afraid to bless communion (called the sacrament) because I didn't know if my priesthood was working that day. Yet if I didn't participate in the ordinances, I would stand out as the single unworthy member of the ward.

This fear followed me when I went on my mission. People would ask for priesthood blessings, and I would hesitate. If we weren't worthy of the priesthood, our declarations of healing would not work. It was whispered that evoking the priesthood when we weren't worthy could even warrant damnation. I discovered that when blessings of healing failed, the recipients could be blamed if they did not have enough faith to be healed. Regardless, lack of a desired result was always the fault of the people involved, and never of the priesthood itself.

Because I held the priesthood, I believed that God expected more from me. I had been given greater light and responsibility, and if I sinned against it, I would receive greater damnation. Doctrine and Covenants 82:3 says, "For of him unto whom much is given much is required; and he who sins against the greater light shall receive the greater condemnation."

Mormon men who hold the priesthood are put on a pedestal. They are expected to be strong for their families and ensure that everyone stays on the covenant path. In reality, they are caught in the middle of a dilemma. The priesthood cannot be used if there is any degree of unrighteous dominion or pride, yet this is a condition of humanity (Romans 3:10) – a sin nature from which we cannot entirely escape.

The priesthood is a double snare. It keeps members from seriously considering Christianity, and it also keeps men tied down to a toxic perfectionism and a veneer of outward righteousness. They become like the Pharisees of old, of whom Jesus said are like whitewashed tombs that indeed appear beautiful outwardly, but inside are full of dead men's bones and all uncleanness (Matthew 23:27).

Missionary Work

Concerning missionary work, *PMG* says, "When people are baptized, they make a covenant to always stand as witnesses of God. They are commanded to share the gospel with those who have not yet received it."[100]

In Mormonism, whenever missionary work is brought up, all anyone talks about are the blessings associated with it. But whenever the word "commandment" is brought up, it comes with an ominous feeling of duty mingled with regret. How many friends did I have who didn't even know I was LDS? I lived in a small town, and no other Mormons went to my high school. It was my fault if they didn't know about the true church.

God didn't intend for me merely to keep *some* of the commandments. I needed to keep them all if I was going to return to His presence in the celestial kingdom.[101] Those who weren't valiant were sent to a lower level of heaven called the terrestrial kingdom, where they would be forever separated from the Father's presence.[102] It made sense because the baptismal covenant said I needed to stand as a witness of God at all times and in all places that I might be in.[103]

I was only a witness to God sometimes, usually as the result of the missionaries visiting my family and asking us to prayerfully consider a friend whom we could allow them to teach. Once I became a missionary, I employed that tactic all the time. People were far more likely to give the Church a fair hearing if someone they knew and trusted was a member.

Missionary work was so important to my family that I felt as if I didn't have the choice not to serve a two-year mission. I attempted to join the army instead, but my mom wouldn't

---

100 *Preach My Gospel*, 88.
101 According to the LDS interpretation of Matthew 5:48.
102 Doctrine and Covenants 76:79.
103 Mosiah 18:9 (Book of Mormon).

have it. She said she would be thrilled if I joined the military, but a mission took precedence.

When I went to serve in Anaheim, California, I discovered that a lot of the missionaries didn't want to be there. One of my companions said that his girlfriend wouldn't marry him if he didn't go, which was a common vow among LDS women. In their eyes, a man who neglected to serve a mission didn't take his faith seriously and wasn't marriage material. Another companion confessed that he prayed whether or not to serve and had received a revelation not to go. The pressure from the culture was so great that he went anyway.

In the middle of my service, a man I had baptized months earlier called to say that he had asked out a woman from the ward and was rejected because he had not served a mission. He was twenty-six when we baptized him and was ineligible to serve. Clearly the repercussions of shirking missionary service are so great that it is hardly a choice at all. Not doing so could make someone an outcast of the faith, hinder his dating prospects, and even harm his ability to get a job if he lived somewhere with a heavy Mormon population.

Eternal Marriage

Eternal marriage is the next item on the long list of religious demands imposed on faithful Mormons. The concept of eternal family is one avenue the missionaries will use to entice people into joining their Church. They will claim that only their priesthood can guarantee that your family will stay together in heaven – and don't you want to live forever with your family? Such a strong emotional pull attracts many people to the Church and keeps them in bondage indefinitely. *PMG* says this about marriage: "Marriage, however, can be eternal only when authorized priesthood holders perform the sealing ordinance in sacred temples and when husbands and wives who have been sealed together keep the covenants they have made."[104]

A forever marriage sounds amazing, but there are damaging aspects to it too. For example, not everyone in Mormonism is capable of finding a spouse. The LDS Church has come out and said that everyone who did not have the chance in mortality will have the opportunity to marry after the resurrection. But the teaching on eternal families is such a sticking point that members without spouses can feel like failures in a religion that idolizes family above all else.

This was certainly the case for me. I was extremely awkward around women and did not have a girlfriend until my mid-twenties. I was convinced that I would never be married, and as a result, my fate was to become an angel in the service of God rather than a god myself.[105]

Greater problems come into play after a couple is sealed in the temple, especially when it comes to leaving the faith. If a person removes their records from the Church, their eternal sealing is undone. Since the LDS Church is the foundation the marriage was built upon, the marriage begins to seem as if it has no anchor and that it is not legitimate at all.

An apostate spouse is also worthless in helping one's mate ascend to godhood in the celestial kingdom. So when one partner abandons ship, there is a new elephant in the room – the unspoken assumption that the faithful partner will be married to someone else in the next life, someone who took the covenants seriously.

This is the dilemma I found myself in after leaving the Church. My marriage didn't feel real. I tried to rekindle it, but for nine years it had grown out of the rocky soil of the Church,

---

104   *Preach My Gospel*, 89.

105   Spencer W. Kimball, "The Importance of Celestial Marriage," *Ensign*, October 1979, https://www.churchofjesuschrist.org/study/ensign/1979/10/the-importance-of-celestial-marriage?lang=eng.

and now that foundation was gone. Within two years of my leaving the Church, my wife decided that the marriage didn't mean anything, and she filed for divorce.

This is not an uncommon occurrence with ex-Mormons. Family ties become strained all around. Mormon parents become agitated because their eternal family is falling apart, and the one who leaves is treated as if he betrayed his loved ones. This simple fact alone explains why it is difficult to leave the LDS faith. It is almost guaranteed that the person who leaves will lose family relationships, and we need to be aware of that when discussing the gospel with missionaries. They have families back home that are determining their worth based on their mission performances.

Even with active members who have not done anything as drastic as leaving the Church, eternal marriage can be a source of stress. If one spouse is not as faithful as the other, and only one of them is attending the temple on a regular basis, there can still be a feeling that they may not make it to exaltation together.

Temples and Family History

The next section of Lesson 5 focuses heavily on a major idol of the LDS faith. Ultimately, every topic this chapter addresses points back to the temple. In the temple, Mormons covenant to keep God's commandments, which defaults to all LDS ordinances and practices. In Mormonism, the temple acts as a sequel to the role of the cross. A Mormon's ability to enter is a litmus test for their worthiness to achieve the highest heaven – the celestial kingdom. The rites performed within are ultimately what allow them to be sealed to their families and obtain exaltation, or to be joint heirs with Christ. In the Mormon mindset, the temple unlocks even greater eternal rewards than what we can receive through the cross.

A lot is required for members to be able to attend the temple. They must prove their worthiness to their local leaders by answering questions in an interview. They must affirm that they pay 10 percent of their income as tithing, that they abstain from tea, coffee, and alcohol, and that they are obeying the commandments.

Missionaries talk about the temple with a great deal of reverence. They will say that it makes sense that God would restore temples since He never changes. If there were temples in Old Testament times, why shouldn't there be temples today? In addition to that, they will share subjective experiences and tell you about how they found peace in the temple or that God revealed something to them there. Be careful about how you handle this subject. The temple is considered sacred, so if your words are perceived as mockery, the conversation will end.

The missionaries will say that in temples, special ordinances are provided that allow people to be like God if they keep the covenants associated with them. Latter-day Saints perform these ordinances vicariously for those who have passed on without a knowledge of the LDS gospel, which is consistent for a religion that requires these ordinances in order to enter into the Father's presence. *PMG* says this:

> The Savior loves all people and desires their salvation. Yet millions of people have died without having any opportunity to hear the message of the restored gospel of Jesus Christ or receive saving ordinances. Through His loving grace and mercy, the Lord makes salvation possible for everyone who did not have the opportunity to receive, understand, and obey the gospel during their mortal lives. The gospel is preached to these deceased people in the spirit world. Members of the Church

on earth perform the saving ordinances in behalf
of their deceased ancestors and others. Deceased
persons living in the spirit world have the opportunity to accept or reject the gospel and the ordinances performed in their behalf.[106]

I have already discussed some of the issues with temples, but
there is more going on here. First, many young members are not
thrilled about doing genealogy work in order to try to locate their
dead ancestors. In my experience growing up Mormon, it was the
older members who generally took the time to search archives
to find ancestors who had not been baptized or sealed to their
spouses. I would feel guilty whenever someone shared the following quote from Joseph Smith: "The greatest responsibility in
this world that God has laid upon us is to seek after our dead."[107]

My mom and grandma were huge genealogy nerds and claimed
to have our line traced all the way back to Adam. However, I
could not care less about genealogy work; yet Joseph Smith said
it was the greatest responsibility we had. None of my peers were
invested in it either. In fact, I'm willing to bet that your young
missionaries cannot trace their pedigrees back five generations.

The LDS Church expects its members to attend the temple
on a regular basis, and a lot of members go monthly. In regions
that are heavily populated with Mormons, there is usually a
temple nearby. I grew up in Austin, and it was a lifesaver when
the San Antonio temple opened up, shaving six hours off a
round trip to the Houston temple.

A temple endowment is a ceremony where Mormons make
a covenant to God or on behalf of the dead. These meetings last
about two hours. When you consider drive time and the cost of

---

106 *Preach My Gospel*, 90.

107 *Teachings of the Presidents of the Church: Joseph Smith* (Salt Lake City: The
Church of Jesus Christ of Latter-day Saints, 2011), 475, https://www.churchofje-
suschrist.org/study/manual/teachings-joseph-smith/chapter-41?lang=eng.

a babysitter to watch your children, that is a significant commitment of time and money. Men and women are separated on opposite sides of the room in an endowment ceremony, yet many Mormon couples consider this their date night!

When the topic of the temple is brought up by members from the pulpit on Sundays, it summons a sense of awe. A hushed silence falls over the room as people reverently think about their holy structure. Growing up, I would hear people say they visited the temple and found peace amid their chaotic lives. It was supposed to be God's house, the place where we could come closest to God and have our prayers answered. Yet it was so sacred that the details of what went on inside were never spoken of, even among other members.

I had no idea what I was getting into when I went into the temple before serving my mission. I was stunned when I entered my first endowment ceremony. We were given strange white ritual clothing to wear and engaged in handshakes and key words that we needed to memorize in order to pass by the sentinels in heaven. Before the ceremony, we were told that we would be making covenants, or promises to God, and that if we didn't feel comfortable making them, we could leave. Because of the pressure from my family, leaving was not an option, so I committed to temple covenants before I knew what they were.

Latter-day Saints make covenants in the temple to live chaste lives, to obey the commandments, and to dedicate their time, talents, and everything else the Lord has blessed them with for building up and defending the LDS Church.

In short, these are promises that no Latter-day Saint can keep, yet the Church places higher guilt on those who break their covenants. When I was Mormon, there were times I wished I hadn't made covenants in the first place because I was not always obedient. I think a lot of Latter-day Saints lie to themselves to silence their consciences about attending the temple. During temple interviews with their bishops, they say they are worthy, and they do their best to put on a show of righteousness, but inwardly that voice of condemnation is always present.

Service

If you ask your average Mormon what is so great about the LDS Church, they will boast of how they assist people in need after disaster strikes. If someone in a congregation needs to move, a significant portion of the men will come and help. Even the local leaders pour in hours of service without receiving compensation of any sort. It sounds like a utopia, but typically these deeds are done out of obligation to a covenant. In Mormonism, good works are part of the path to salvation. *PMG* says, "One of the great blessings of membership in the Church is the opportunity to serve. When we give loving service to others, we are serving God. When we are baptized, we covenant to give such service."[108]

At the moment of baptism, Mormons promise, among other things, to serve others. If they keep their end of the bargain, God's part is to grant eternal life. This bargain is a sad one because it hinges on the person succeeding in obeying Mormon commandments – obeying extrabiblical commandments and covenants, doing missionary work, and carrying others' burdens. Therefore, if a Latter-day Saint is not faithful in these endeavors, there is no guarantee of eternal life.[109] Serving becomes mandatory labor that merits salvation instead of being a gift freely given out of love.

Part of service is receiving what is referred to as a "calling." The bishop pulls someone aside and gives them a special job in the Church that they must fulfill, without compensation, for the good of the congregation. There have been many callings

---

108   *Preach My Gospel*, 91.
109   Doctrine and Covenants 82:10.

I have received that I did not want and that had nothing to do with my skill set. For example, when my first wife and I were newly married, we were called to assist in the nursery. Two- and three-year-olds were not my forte – not to mention that my bride and I hadn't learned to communicate yet. It ended up causing a significant amount of stress in our marriage.

Despite the hardship, it was unthinkable to ask to be assigned to something else. To question the local leadership was to question the Lord Himself. After all, it was God who really chose everyone's callings. If the calling was a good fit, it was because the Lord needed that person's talents. If it was a bad fit, it was because the Lord wanted that person to grow. It never crossed my mind that the leadership wasn't inspired or that they were controlling us with these callings.

At one point, I was called into the Presidency of the Elder's Quorum, which is the auxiliary over the men in the congregation. I was required to attend a meeting every Wednesday night after work, which usually went late into the night. Mind you, this was without any sort of compensation. Some callings are even worse! Mormon bishops have so much responsibility that it is the equivalent of a full-time job. Since they aren't compensated, they must work a real job on top of that, all at the expense of their family time.

There are often talks given at church about how members need to magnify their callings. They need to find ways to excel at whatever the Lord asks them to do. That means there is always more time Mormons can pour into serving the Church. In addition to that, each family is assigned a turn in a rotation to clean the church building on Saturday mornings. If someone is moving, the men are pressured into helping with it. In retrospect, I realize that the Mormon Church kept me too busy to think about whether it was true. I was always too hurried from one service project to the next.

Enduring to the End

The cherry on top of the LDS gospel of amputation is the prospect of enduring to the end. But how does a Mormon do that when they cannot even keep all their covenants for a week? The answer is repentance. *PMG* explains enduring to the end like this: "As we continue to exercise faith in Christ, repent, and renew our covenants, we enjoy continued guidance from the Holy Ghost. If we endure to the end of our lives in being true to our covenants, we will receive exaltation."[110]

LDS Church President Russell M. Nelson taught:

> Keep on the covenant path. Your commitment to follow the Savior by making covenants with Him and then keeping those covenants will open the door to every spiritual blessing and privilege available to men, women, and children everywhere. . . . The end for which each of us strives is to be endowed with power in a house of the Lord, sealed as families, faithful to the covenants made in a temple that qualify us for the greatest gift of God – that of eternal life.[111]

> A few members do not endure or remain fully active. However, enduring to the end is a personal responsibility. We are to work out our own salvation.

Let's dissect this statement to determine what enduring to the end means. First, the LDS members must keep their covenants throughout their lives in order to obtain exaltation. When

---

110   *Preach My Gospel*, 93.

111   Russell M. Nelson, "As We Go Forward Together," *Ensign*, April 2018, https://www.churchofjesuschrist.org/study/ensign/2018/04/as-we-go-forward-together?lang=eng.

they slip up, they must renew their covenants, either through repentance or by taking communion on Sunday.

If you ask your missionaries how often they repent, they will probably confess that they do it weekly or even daily. This is strikingly similar to how early Jews had to continuously offer sin offerings because they could only cover their sins for a short time. Repentance is one of the great lies of the LDS Church. It is designed to give its members the false hope that they can eventually overcome sin themselves.[112]

When I would sin as a Latter-day Saint, I would console myself by assuming there was plenty of time to repent. When I tried to repent but found myself still sinning later, I would think that perfection did not matter at that moment. As long as I was improving, no matter how gradually, I believed that I could still get by with grace. But when years passed and I couldn't see an improvement, it began to dawn on me that I couldn't be righteous.

Of course, I believed in a spirit world in which repentance could continue until the second coming – similar to the Catholic view of purgatory. The LDS Church always taught that it was harder to repent in the spirit world and that the best time to do so was during life on earth.[113] Like most Mormons, I mastered the art of faking righteousness, but inwardly there was a storm of doubt that could not be quelled. I knew I wasn't worthy of the celestial kingdom, and I feared that I never would be. I always pictured myself letting God down on judgment day and watching my family enter the highest heaven without me because I wasn't valiant enough. That thought haunted me for most of my life.

Communion (known as the sacrament) acts as a way for Mormons to hit the refresh button on their covenants and start the week with a clean slate. However, the leaders are very clear that

---

112   Jeffrey R. Holland, "Be Ye Therefore Perfect – Eventually," General Conference of the Church of Jesus Christ of Latter-day Saints, October 2017, 40-42, https://www.churchofjesuschrist.org/study/general-conference/2017/10/be-ye-therefore-perfect-eventually?lang=eng.

113   Alma 34:34 (Book of Mormon).

members are not to take the sacrament unworthily. I understood "unworthily" to mean that if I was struggling with sin, I should not take the emblems of the sacrament. In fact, after confessing sin, I have had bishops admonish me *not* to take the sacrament until after I had gained control over the sin that had me in its clutches. There is such a difference between LDS communion and Christian communion! As a Mormon, I never knew the joy of partaking of in communion as scripture portrays it, in remembrance of Christ. It was always an offering that I needed to present from a place of purity, or else I believed that God might not accept it.

Everything in Mormonism painted a picture of a detached, wrathful God. While on my mission, I believed that God would not hear or answer my prayers if my apartment was dirty. If I tried to give a blessing and no inspiration came, it was because I was unworthy. If I wanted God's blessings, I had to rid myself of sin first because He didn't want to get His hands dirty. If I wanted God's presence, I needed to visit a holy place, such as a temple.

My religion was not about God reaching out to take hold of me, but it was about me reaching up to grab God's hand. However, no matter how much I tried, I could never reach anything until I fell into grace. It was as if I had been wandering around in the desert my whole life, spurred on by mirages that turned out to be shifting sand – until I stumbled across an oasis with a crystal lake of cool, clean water that never ran dry.

The LDS missionaries may try to resist the true, biblical gospel message, but as someone who once stood in their shoes, I can tell you there is nothing they desire more.

Pointing Out the Two Gospels

If you ask the missionaries if they would drink something that had the tiniest bit of alcohol in it, they will surely balk at the idea. Their scripture condemns drinking alcohol, and even a tiny bit corrupts the whole drink. Explain that this is why you cannot accept the gospel of works. Even if the missionaries are only claiming that you need baptism to go to heaven, that still discredits grace and contaminates the gospel.

Drive this point home with Romans 11:5-6: *Even so then, at this present time there is a remnant according to the election of grace. And if by grace, then it is no longer of works; otherwise grace is no longer grace. But if it is of works, it is no longer grace: otherwise work is no longer work.*

The message Paul is conveying here is that grace does not function when works are involved. When it comes to salvation, it is one or the other. If we rely on even one iota of obedience to save us, there is no grace that makes up the difference. We are left on our own. Whether the missionaries concede the point or not, they should at least agree that you believe a vastly different gospel than they do.

Then point out Galatians 1:8: *But even if we, or an angel from heaven, preach any other gospel to you than what we have preached to you, let him be accursed.* Now that it has been established that there are two gospels on the table, tell the missionaries that one of you is right and one is cursed. That is why discussing the true gospel is so important.

Priesthood Fallacies

The LDS Church claims to have prophets and apostles who are authorized to delegate the use of the priesthood. A large portion of lesson 5 is devoted to teaching an investigator that the apostles held the priesthood in New Testament times, but when they died, the priesthood went with them. They will try to convince you that since their leaders hold the same titles as those found in the ancient church, this is evidence that Christ's church really was lost only to be restored later.

The problem for the LDS missionaries is that the biblical gospel negates the need for mortal leaders to stand as mediators between God and man. For proof, we only need to go to Hebrews chapter 7, which explains that Jesus is a better priest than what the law offered. Then it gives a number of reasons why (Hebrews 7:1-19). First, the priests were mortal, but Jesus is eternal:

> *Also there were many priests, because they were prevented by death from continuing. But He, because He continues forever, has an unchangeable priesthood. Therefore He is also able to save to the uttermost those who come to God through Him, since He always lives to make intercession for them.* (Hebrews 7:23-25)

Second, the priests were sinful, but Jesus is holy:

> *For such a High Priest was fitting for us, who is holy, harmless, undefiled, separate from sinners, and has become higher than the heavens; who does not need daily, as those high priests, to offer up sacrifices, first for His own sins and then for the people's, for this He did once for all when He offered up Himself.* (Hebrews 7:26-27)

Coincidentally, these arguments also exalt Jesus above the LDS priesthood leaders. After all, don't LDS priesthood holders die? Doesn't their priesthood have to constantly be passed down from generation to generation to keep it alive? Surely a never-ending priesthood by an eternal God is better than that.

Also, don't LDS priesthood leaders sin? Don't they take the sacrament each week to renew their own covenants? The picture Hebrews paints of the priest sacrificing for his own sin first is a perfect parallel of what happens in an LDS ward when communion is passed. The bishop takes the sacrament first; then it is passed to the rest of the members.

Hebrews 10:11-14 states further:

> *And every priest stands ministering daily and offering repeatedly the same sacrifices, which can never take away sins. But this Man, after He had offered one sacrifice for sins forever, sat down at the right hand of God, from that time waiting till His enemies are made His footstool. For by one offering He has perfected forever those who are being sanctified.*

The Jews had to make numerous offerings for sin because these offerings only provided a temporary covering for sin. After explaining this to the missionaries, ask them how often they repent. They will most likely say that they repent daily, signifying that they have the same problem the ancient Jews did. All they get is a temporary reprieve from sin; otherwise, there would be no need to keep asking for forgiveness.

It should also be noted that the Greek word for "sanctified" in Hebrews 10:14 is present tense and represents a continuing process. That is why the NKJV (and other versions) translate it as *those who are being sanctified*. The missionaries will probably interpret it as saying we are only perfect *after* sanctification is completed, but Hebrews places perfection before sanctification. Take them back to Hebrews 7:25 and remind them that Jesus saves *to the uttermost*. From that statement we can infer three things:

1. Jesus is able to make us completely worthy, even while we are occupied with our struggle against sin.

2. Priesthood leaders and saving ordinances play no role in salvation because Jesus leaves no void to fill.

3. While scripture does speak of rewards in heaven, there
   is only one level of salvation. We are either saved or we
   are not.

Mormon Rebuttal #1: Grace Is a License to Sin

At some point in the conversation, the missionary may say
something like, "So do you believe obedience doesn't matter
and you can sin all you want?"

If this happens, don't get upset. This question needs to be
handled with patience and love. After all, this is simply how
an unregenerate heart sees grace. It is just their self-centered
worldview shining through. Don't see it as an accusation, but
as a reminder of the terrible predicament they are in.

Ask them this question in response: "If someone loved you
unconditionally, would it be your goal to betray them as much
as possible?" This should stop them in their tracks. Obviously,
no one with a shred of decency would take advantage of someone so dedicated to them.

Explain to the missionaries that true Christians take obedience
to God very seriously. Tell them that once salvation is given, we
must desire to please God. Our obedience is a symptom of love,
not a currency to earn heaven. Share Romans 13:8-10 with them:

> *Owe no one anything except to love one another: for
> he who loves another has fulfilled the law. For the
> commandments, "You shall not commit adultery,"
> "You shall not murder," "You shall not steal," "You
> shall not bear false witness," "You shall not covet,"
> and if there is any other commandment, are all
> summed up in this saying, namely, "You shall love
> your neighbor as yourself." Love does no harm to a
> neighbor; therefore love is the fulfillment of the law.*

Follow up with this question: If loving our neighbor naturally results in us wanting to keep the law, wouldn't loving God do the same?

Mormon Rebuttal #2: There Is Always More

The missionaries may concede that salvation comes through faith alone, but they will say that it only gets you to the terrestrial kingdom. To gain eternal life in the highest heaven, you must be baptized. To be exalted, you must be sealed to a spouse.

We must stand firm in the fact that salvation comes through Christ alone. In order to convince the missionaries of this, you will need to explain how God saves us.

I like to use LDS temples as a jumping-off point. In Mormon theology, the dead cannot partake in the saving ordinances, so living benefactors attend the temple and provide ordinances for them vicariously. The dead person merely accepts the ordinance, and it is accredited to their account as if they participated in it. This is called imputation.

In Christianity, the cross is even better than an LDS temple. Since we couldn't obey God's law perfectly, Jesus lived obediently on our behalf and offered His righteousness to us vicariously on the cross. This is why Paul promotes a righteousness that is not his own (Philippians 3:9), while Romans 5:10 associates salvation not only with Christ's death, but also with His life: *For if when we were enemies we were reconciled to God through the death of His Son, much more, having been reconciled, we shall be saved by His life.*

Ask the missionaries if Jesus is worthy of all the blessings that the Father has in store. They should answer that He is. Assert that it naturally follows that if we are given Christ's righteousness, there is nothing more for us to obtain.

They might say that God gives His righteousness out a little at a time. If this happens, explain that infinity cannot be divided. If Jesus gives us 1 percent of His righteousness, that amount is still infinite. Therefore, we can reasonably assume that we are worthy of salvation, eternal life, and exaltation all in the same instant.

Mormon Rebuttal #3: We Receive Grace through Baptism by the Proper Authority

Now that you have established the fact that grace saves to the utmost, the missionaries will say we must do something to merit that grace – namely, being baptized by someone who holds priesthood authority. Baptism is so iconic in Mormonism that salvation tied to faith sinks their battleship. To faithful Latter-day Saints, baptism is the moment they enter a covenant for eternal life and are adopted into Christ.[114] Baptism is the pedestal on which their idol of priesthood sits. If you are looking for a point of attack, this is it.

Point the missionaries to Romans 8:16-17: *The Spirit Himself bears witness with our spirit that we are children of God, and if children, then heirs – heirs of God and joint heirs with Christ, if indeed we suffer with Him, that we may also be glorified together.*

You have already established that there is nothing left to earn when grace saves us, and this verse reiterates that. If we are children of God, then we are joint heirs with Christ. Thus, adoption is not the beginning of a path, but it is the final destination. To say otherwise is to make our dominion greater than Christ's.

So the big question is, When do we become children of God? Point the missionaries to Romans 8:14: *For as many as are led by the Spirit of God, these are sons of God.*

---

114   Mosiah 5:7-8 (Book of Mormon).

Now ask this question: Are people led by the Spirit before entering the baptismal font? The Mormons will concede that this is the case. Tell them that according to Romans 8, if the Spirit leads us, we are joint heirs with Christ prior to being baptized.

I recommend taking the missionaries through the following passages: John 1:12-13, Galatians 3:26, James 2:23, and Romans 4:3. These verses clearly state that we become children of God through belief and that righteousness was imputed to Abraham when he believed God. Then read Romans 4:20-24 with them:

> *He did not waver at the promise of God through*
> *unbelief, but was strengthened in faith, giving glory*
> *to God, and being fully convinced that what He had*
> *promised He was also able to perform. And there-*
> *fore "it was accounted to him for righteousness."*
> *Now it was not written for his sake alone that it was*
> *imputed to him, but also for us. It shall be imputed*
> *to us who believe in Him who raised up Jesus our*
> *Lord from the dead.*

These passages place imputation and adoption squarely on faith. If you have laid the groundwork properly, there is no squirming out of it.

Closing the Deal

Ask the missionaries to envision how their families would react if they announced their departure from the Church. Ask the elders how this reaction would affect them. Be patient and hear them through to the end. This exercise is important because it brings the idea of leaving to their minds and forces them to consider it seriously.

After they have given you their thoughts, testify that Jesus is worth losing everything for – even family relationships. Share Matthew 10:34-39:

> *Do not think that I came to bring peace on earth. I did not come to bring peace but a sword. For I have come to "set a man against his father, a daughter against her mother, and a daughter-in-law against her mother-in-law"; and "a man's enemies will be those of his own household." He who loves father or mother more than Me is not worthy of Me. And he who loves son or daughter more than Me is not worthy of Me. And he who does not take his cross and follow after Me is not worthy of Me. He who finds his life will lose it, and he who loses his life for My sake will find it.*

Jesus did not come to seal families, but to tear them apart. That is the bad news. The good news is that we are sealed together in the marriage between Christ and His church. Our new eternal family is every believer in Christ. Mark 10:29-30 states:

> *So Jesus answered and said, "Assuredly, I say to you, there is no one who has left house or brothers or sisters or father or mother or wife or children or lands, for My sake and the gospel's, who shall not receive a hundredfold now in this time – houses and brothers and sisters and mothers and children and lands, with persecutions – and in the age to come, eternal life."*

Jesus reaffirmed this in Matthew 12:48-50, when He was told that His mother and brothers wanted to talk to Him:

But He answered and said to the one who told Him,
"Who is My mother and who are My brothers?" And
He stretched out His hand toward His disciples and
said, "Here are My mother and My brothers! For
whoever does the will of My Father in heaven is My
brother and sister and mother."

Explain that Jesus made a purposeful distinction between His blood relatives and His family. We are part of a great family when we do God's will. And what is His will? Jesus answers that question in John 6:40: *This is the will of Him who sent Me, that everyone who sees the Son and believes in Him may have everlasting life; and I will raise him up at the last day.*

It would be good to ask the missionaries if they would still be excited to go to heaven if their families wouldn't be there, but Jesus Christ would still be there. Is Jesus enough for them?

Finally, explain to them what an earnest is. I had some missionaries over one night and used the example of buying a house. An earnest is money given to guarantee that you will pay the rest later. I told them that God has already given believers the earnest of their inheritance: the Holy Spirit. They had never heard such a thing. I shared Ephesians 1:13-14 (KJV): *In whom ye also trusted, after that ye heard the word of truth, the gospel of your salvation: in whom also after that ye believed, ye were sealed with that holy Spirit of promise, which is the earnest of our inheritance until the redemption of the purchased possession, unto the praise of his glory.*

Our High Priest

There is one word that undoes all the heresy and all the abuse of the LDS Church. There is one word that lights up the darkness and provides a ray of hope. That word is the majestic name of

Jesus. Everything the LDS Church preaches is made null and void by what Jesus Christ does and who He is. The need for eternal marriage is nullified because Jesus is our bridegroom. The temples are obsolete because Jesus imputes His righteousness vicariously on the cross. Enduring to the end ceases to be man's responsibility and becomes a work of God. We cannot be lost because Christ holds us in the palm of His hand. Although we may wander, He leaves the ninety-nine and brings His lost sheep back into the fold (Matthew 18:12).

The book of Hebrews calls Jesus our High Priest. This sentiment is lost on the LDS, but the Jews would have understood that there was no more need for a man to make intercession for them, nor was there need for a temple.

To put it in LDS terms, Jesus is our bishop. We do not need to confess our sins to a man because we can confess them to Christ. Jesus is our prophet, so we no longer need to place ourselves under the authority of LDS leaders. Jesus is our proxy. We no longer need to do works to merit salvation because our work has already been done. Jesus is our eternal family, our priesthood, and our temple. We can throw out our idols and trust that His grace is sufficient to catch us and carry us home.

* * * *

Michael Flournoy grew up as a seventh-generation Latter-day Saint, descended from Mormon pioneers and polygamists. As a member, he wrote *A Biblical Defense of Mormonism* (2012) and engaged in a number of public debates against Christians, including a debate against Lynn Wilder on *UnBelievable?* He is the author of *Falling into Grace: How a Mormon Apologist Stumbled into Christianity* (2020). Michael and his family reside in Texas.

Appendix: Resources

Understanding Mormonism

- Institute for Religious Research - mit.irr.org
- *The Saints of Zion: An Introduction to Mormon Theology*, Travis Kerns. B & H Academic, 2018.
- *Speaking the Truth in Love to Mormons*, Mark J. Cares. Truth in Love Ministry, 2013.
- *Understanding Your Mormon Neighbor: A Quick Christian Guide for Relating to Latter-day Saints*, Ross Anderson. Zondervan, 2011.

Evangelism to Latter-day Saints

- Truth in Love Ministry - tilm.org
- Adam's Road Ministry - www.adamsroadministry.com
- *Introducing Christianity to Mormons: A Practical and Comparative Guide to What the Bible Teaches*, Eric Johnson. Harvest House, 2022.
- *Crossing the Chasm: Helping Mormons Discover the Bridge to God*, Mark J. Cares & Jon Leach. Truth in Love Ministries, 2021.

- *Engaging with Mormons: Understanding their World; Sharing Good News,* Corey Miller. The Good Book Company, 2020.

- *Sharing the Good News with Mormons: Practical Strategies for Getting the Conversation Started,* Eric Johnson & Sean McDowell, eds. Harvest House, 2018.

- *I Love Mormons: A New Way to Share Christ with Latter-day Saints,* David L. Rowe. Baker, 2005

Apologetics Related to Mormonism

- Mormonism Research Ministry - www.mrm.org

- Christian Apologetics and Research Ministry - carm.org/world-religions/mormonism

- *Answering Mormons' Questions: Ready Responses for Inquiring Latter-day Saints,* Bill McKeever & Eric Johnson. Kregel Publications, 2012

Discipling Former Latter-day Saints

- Faith After Mormonism - faithaftermormonism.org

- The Outer Brightness Podcast: From Mormon to Jesus - www.outerbrightnesspodcast.com

- The Unveiling Grace Podcast: Experience a Grace that Heals - unveilinggracepodcast.com

- *Jesus Without Joseph: Following Christ After Leaving Mormonism: A Study Guide,* Ross Anderson. Independently published, 2015.

- *Starting at the Finish Line: The Gospel of Grace for Mormons,* John B. Wallace. Pomona House, 2014.

- *Out of the Cults and Into the Church: Understanding and Encouraging Ex-Cultists*, Janis Hutchinson. Kregel Resources, 1994

Stories of Former Mormons Coming to Faith in Christ

- *Passport to Heaven: The True Story of a Zealous Mormon Missionary Who Discovers the Jesus He Never Knew*, Micah Wilder. Harvest House, 2021.

- *Falling Into Grace: How a Mormon Apologist Stumbled Into Christianity,* Michael Flournoy. Independently published, 2020.

- *Out of Zion: Meeting Jesus in the Shadow of the Mormon Temple*, Lisa Brockman. Harvest House, 2019.

- *Leaving Mormonism: Why Four Scholars Changed Their Minds*, Corey Miller and Lynn K. Wilder, eds. Kregel, 2017.

- *A Mormon's Unexpected Journey: Finding the Grace I Never Knew*, Carma Naylor. Light of Truth Books, 2014.

- *Mormonism, the Matrix, and Me: My Journey from Kolob to Calvary*, Tracy Tennant. Right Track Publications, 2014.

- *Unveiling Grace*, Lynn K. Wilder. Zondervan, 2013

- *Out of Mormonism: A Woman's True Story*, Judy Robertson. Bethany House, 2011.